PASSING THE TORCH

Since 1996, Bloomberg Press has published books for financial professionals, as well as books of general interest in investing, economics, current affairs, and policy affecting investors and business people. Titles are written by well-known practitioners, BLOOMBERG NEWS® reporters and columnists, and other leading authorities and journalists. Bloomberg Press books have been translated into more than 20 languages.

For a list of available titles, please visit our website at www.wiley.com/go/bloombergpress.

PASSING THE TORCH

Preserving Family Wealth Beyond
the Third Generation

Ilze Alberts

WILEY

Published by John Wiley & Sons, Inc., Hoboken, New Jersey.
Published simultaneously in Canada.

For general information on our other products and services or for technical support, please contact our Customer Care Department within the United States at (800) 762–2974, outside the United States at (317) 572–3993, or fax (317) 572–4002.

Wiley publishes in a variety of print and electronic formats and by print-on-demand. Some material included with standard print versions of this book may not be included in e-books or in print-on-demand. If this book refers to media such as a CD or DVD that is not included in the version you purchased, you may download this material at http://booksupport.wiley.com. For more information about Wiley products, visit www.wiley.com.

Library of Congress Cataloging-in-Publication Data

Names: Alberts, Ilze, 1958- author.
Title: Passing the torch : preserving family wealth beyond the third
   generation / by Ilze Alberts.
Description: Hoboken, New Jersey : John Wiley & Sons, Inc., [2018] | Includes
   index. |
Identifiers: LCCN 2017059968 (print) | LCCN 2018010658 (ebook) | ISBN
   9781119486459 (pdf) | ISBN 9781119486435 (epub) | ISBN 9781119486442
   (cloth)
Subjects: LCSH: Finance, Personal. | Families. | Wealth. | Estate planning.
Classification: LCC HG179 (ebook) | LCC HG179 .A399 2018 (print) | DDC
   332.024/016—dc23
LC record available at https://lccn.loc.gov/2017059968

Cover Design: Wiley
Cover Image: © BestPix / Shutterstock

Printed in the United States of America

10 9 8 7 6 5 4 3 2 1

Ignite and pass the torch. Unlock the high net worth in every family member for the ultimate prosperity and fulfillment of the family for generations to come.

I dedicate this book to my fellow torch igniter, Roelf Alberts, and our children we are passing the torch to: Charne, Jacques, and Louis-Franz. May it shine brightly on your path.

Contents

CONTENTS

Foreword

by James Hughes

It is my privilege to join Ilze Alberts' journey as she imparts the wisdom of her deeply lived life of commitment to helping families and the individuals who compose them thrive and flourish.

In the book you are about to enter, Ilze offers you the gift of her awareness of what has helped families avoid the entropy that leads to their early dissolution in three or less generations and what those few families do who thrive and flourish beyond three generations.

She will share with you that it is in the great virtues of family harmony, family support of individual dreams toward all family boats rising, and family defining itself as its positive connections of affinity $1 + 1 = 3$, that a family discovers and sustains its journey to long-term flourishing.

She will help you to appreciate that a family consists of four qualitative (spiritual, social, intellectual, and human capital) and one quantitative (financial) capitals. She will encourage your awareness of a frequently missed truth that a family's long-term success lies in growing the first four and dynamically preserving the fifth as a resource to grow the first four.

She will offer you the wisdom that a family who does not in its second, hopefully its first, generation form the intention, as its highest purpose and ambition, to flourish for many generations to come *cannot* succeed. To break the shirtsleeves-to-shirtsleeves proverb so often true, it must practice that intention through seeking to enhance the journeys of happiness of every family member, toward each having a meaningful life, all toward the whole family flourishing.

Valuably, Ilze brings to the challenge of helping your family flourish a depth of psychological mindedness and awareness of the gifts of positive psychology's developmental practices and assessments that I have not encountered in such abundance elsewhere.

By combining virtue, psychological mindedness, and proven individual family member and whole family developmental practices, Ilze charts the course for your family to flourish for seven generations and beyond.

I have deeply enjoyed my journey with Ilze in her professional life of service to human flourishing, now continued and artfully shared as a gift to all families in *Passing the Torch: Preserving Family Wealth Beyond the Third Generation*.

I have every confidence that as you and your family now accompany her on her journey to help your family flourish through her gift to you of her wisdom and experience; through her helping you imagine your family preserving its wealth, its human, intellectual, social and spiritual self; through her encouraging and informing your endeavors to enhance the journey of happiness of each of your family members, all toward your goal of your whole family flourishing; and by adopting and living out the philosophy Ilze imparts, that yours will be one of the very few families who truly flourishes.

I look forward to greeting you on our pilgrim's way as we walk together with Ilze to accomplish your high worthy purpose, the thriving of each of your family members and the preserving of your family far beyond three generations.

Preface

The purpose of this book is *first* to create awareness in families that it is the birthright of every family to be a powerful unit for generations to come. *Second*, I want this book to create the awareness in families that it is the birthright of every family member, as individuals, to have the opportunity to unlock their highest potential for their ultimate fulfillment, meaning, inspiration, and prosperity. *Third*, bonds of affinity that exist between family members are stronger than blood bonds. It's important to form bonds of affinity if the family is to continue for generations as a powerful family. *Fourth*, it is my heart's desire to assist families for multiple generations to develop the know-how, the skills, and the human behavioral understanding to keep the family vision growing until the momentum of the snowball keeps on to such an extent that the impact and influence of that vision will be felt seven generations from now. *Fifth*, I wish to assist families in becoming inspired to create and maintain a family vision for multiple generations, to empower the family in transforming the proverb from shirtsleeves-to-shirtsleeves in three generations.

From Shirtsleeves-to-Shirtsleeves in Three Generations

In Japan, there's an expression, "Rice paddies to rice paddies in three generations." The Scottish say, "The father buys, the son builds, the grandchild sells, and his son begs." In China, "Wealth never survives three generations." Around the world there are many variations on this theme, all used to describe the tendency of the third generation of a family to squander the wealth obtained by the first generation.

According to studies, only 30 percent of family businesses built by one generation are passed on to their children, and only 10 percent of those businesses ever reach a third generation. One reason suggested is that the third generation doesn't possess the same *set of values, work ethic, and perspective* because of their very different experience growing up.

The first generation struggles hard to rise above their current conditions to achieve a more comfortable life for themselves and their family. They work hard, diligently save their money, and by their later years have something of value to pass on.

Their children, the second generation, grow up as a witness to their parents' struggle and understand the value of hard work. Although they now live a comfortable life, they can remember a childhood filled with frugality and perhaps even poverty. Because of this, they make educational and financial choices that help them build on what their parents created. By retirement, they have, most likely, acquired even greater wealth.

The third generation, however, has no memory of want or struggle. They've only known a life of plenty. When the family wealth is passed onto them, they lack the values and skills necessary to maintain the health of the assets. If universal proverbs and small business statistics are to be believed, the third generation squanders the resources their parents and grandparents worked so hard to achieve. Thus, the three-generations cycle.

Figure 1 shows the etymology of the word *wealth*.

FIGURE 1 Etymology of the word *wealth*

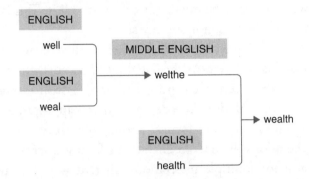

The word wealth in Middle English is welthe, which refers to weal, on the pattern of *health*. Wealth means *well-being* and *prosperity*. It is the right of every person to be prosperous and live with well-being and fulfillment.

It's also the right of every person to have the following opportunities:

- To live an extraordinary and exemplary life and to raise culture and society through it
- To serve vast numbers of people. It is in service to others that meaning of life increases
- To develop a transcendent mindset about money and wealth and to understand the universal principle of fair exchange
- To have access to higher education for mental empowerment
- To have access to specialized health care for optimum health and vitality.

My Story

Changing the predictive outcome that follows the from shirtsleeves-to-shirtsleeves in three generations proverb has taken on tremendous value to me. Why am I doing whatever it takes in an attempt to find out how? It's common knowledge that a void drives a value on something; whatever we perceive to be missing, we strive to fill it. This is certainly true for me, and the reason lies in my story.

My father grew up with wealth yet when he died, he was financially dependent on his children. As the daughter of parents who lost all our family wealth (they were the third generation), I wish to raise awareness, facilitate the mindset, the desire, and the appropriate skills for my children and me to transform the from shirtsleeves-to-shirtsleeves in three generations proverb to enable our family to create and grow family wealth for multiple generations. In that way, we take action to live extraordinary lives that raise the culture we live in and obtain the best opportunities to grow and expand our family for the ultimate fulfillment, well-being, and prosperity of every family member for multiple generations. By doing this, we have a greater opportunity to invest in our world society and contribute to the raising of world standards in education and health. Our wealth can unlock more opportunities for education and health worldwide. Family wealth through generations is not exclusively for the benefit of the family, because it's through the acts of service and unlocking of opportunities for society that family wealth transcends the generational family to become the cosmic family.

We do not resent our parents for the actions and choices they made. I am grateful that through their choices I developed a big void regarding generational wealth. That void has given me a life purpose and meaning. I can use their lack of insight and knowledge as a springboard and through study, research, and practice, I can find inspiring ways to transform the cycle for my family and, in the process, empower my children and their children and their children—for multiple generations.

I'm certain that I'm not the only parent who has asked myself the following question: "I'm spending so much time, energy, and money on my children's mental development by sending them for the best education, but what am I doing to educate them about understanding human behavior and being financially wise?" Acquiring knowledge, understanding human behavior, and being financially skilled and wise will be the three most important influences I can have on the next generation's lives. By sharing the gift of knowledge, human behavior skills, and financial skills and wisdom, I share the gift of empowerment in all areas of life.

True Family Wealth

A family's true wealth consists of:

- *The talents, personalities, and genius of each family member.* There is no higher value in the balance sheet of a family than *human capital.* Each individual family member is an asset (and a liability) and each family member is a valuable source of knowledge, a potential contribution, and an inherent value because of the unique individuality.
- *The family's story, or narrative.* Every family has an origin and a history and the narrative of every family is unique, playing an important role in the development of society worldwide. Each family's narrative is a beautiful and colorful piece of a masterful tapestry. The choices and decisions of your previous generations have a direct impact on your life right now. You come from their choices, decisions, and actions. Your choices, decisions, and actions will equally have an impact on the next generations for years, decades, centuries, millenniums. Who knows how far reaching the effects may be?
- *The mental capital of the family—the mental abilities and exposure to education represented by the family members.* Growing up in a family with the financial means to afford excellent education to the family members contributes to the advancement of the mental capital of the family. The different life experiences, exposure to global experiences through travel, and exposure to knowledge all contribute to wealth of the family's mental capital.
- *Emotional intelligence of the family.* Families with exposure to wealth have more opportunities to develop their emotional intelligence simply because they can afford to pay for mental health services, personal life coaches, and programs and seminars that

teach emotional intelligence. They have exposure to books, online products, international conferences, and tertiary education—all of which help develop their self-confidence and self-esteem. Money does not buy happiness, but money can buy many opportunities for self-development, empowerment, and emotional intelligence.

- *The family's health and vitality.* Physical wealth refers to the opportunity to have optimal health conditions. Good health increases with specialized medical services, a healthy diet, and physical exercise, taking supplements, and the awareness and desire to look after your health. The more educated families are, the more the family's purpose and vision encompasses something bigger than themselves. The more members of the family have a sense of meaning in their lives, the higher the value they place on health and vitality, because the body is treated as the vehicle to take extraordinary service to the world.
- *A* healthy family is a wealthy family.
- *Social network and interactions.* Family members build a network over their lifetimes. Families do not live as islands, and the quality and endurance of social networks and interactions add to the impact and influence of each family member as well as the family as a unit. Like attracts like and the quality of friendships and social networks is a reflection of the endearing characteristics of the family. The lack of quality friendships equally reflects the lack of the family to build endearing friendships with significant people outside of the family bonds.
- *A family's financial wealth.* Family wealth is built by a man (husband, father) or a woman (wife, mother) or by a man and a woman (husband, father and wife, mother) who perceive a big void in their financial well-being and therefore in the financial well-being of their family. This big void acts as the driving force and intrinsic motivation to build wealth for the family. The void, or absence of financial means, becomes the fuel in the family-wealth engine. Money is a form of energy. Money as a form of energy flows where it is valued and appreciated and looked after and where it has a purpose beyond acquiring material things. Once the wealth creator understands the

snowball effect of wealth creation, the wealth being created often takes on a more significant purpose; its purpose becomes bigger than just creating a great life for the family. The wealth creation transforms into a vision and legacy for the family, sometimes for generations. Philanthropy becomes part of the family's outreach into society and the meaning of the family wealth creation lifts up many individuals and families. This is also when the shirtsleeves-to-shirtsleeves in three generations proverb starts to be a factor for the family to consider.

Why Are You Reading This Book?

It's highly likely that you're either the visionary and wealth creator of your family wealth or that you're the next generation and you wish to shift the energy of the shirtsleeves-to-shirtsleeves in three generations proverb. You may also be a professional service provider to high-net-worth families. This book is written with the intention of providing some answers to the big question: how do we change or transform the cycle of the shirtsleeves-to-shirtsleeves proverb? Can we even change it at all? Since energy can't be eliminated, perhaps it can only be transformed.

In his book *Family Wealth*, James Hughes tells us, "Family wealth is not self-perpetuating. Without careful planning and stewardship, a hard-earned fortune can easily be dissipated within a generation or two." He has made a valuable contribution in proposing a theory and method for practicing successful wealth preservation. Throughout my writings, you'll find James Hughes' work has had a significant impact on my way of thinking and understanding the preservation of family wealth. I am deeply grateful for his impact and influence on my understanding and thinking.

Sir Isaac Newton said, "I'd rather stand on the shoulders of giants than in their shadows, for then I can see further." James Hughes is one of the giants on whose shoulders I'm standing to see further. I have indeed spent many hours pondering a possible transformation of the energy of the shirtsleeves-to-shirtsleeves proverb. This book is my contribution to offering possible ways to do that.

Another giant on whose shoulder I'm standing is the human behavior specialist and polymath, Dr. John Demartini. Throughout this book, his impact and influence on my understanding of human behavior will be keenly evident. He has taken my understanding of human behavior where my training as a psychologist could not.

My wish is that the combination of many masterful minds will shine light on the transformation of the energy of the shirtsleeves-to-shirtsleeves proverb.

CHAPTER 1

What You Perceive Is Missing Drives You

Every person has unfulfilled wishes and dreams. As human beings, if we keep on perceiving something is missing, we feel unfulfilled. It's the perception of emptiness, or a void, that becomes the driving force for a person to take some action or perform some service and gives it priority and importance. Without a perception of the void—the feeling that something is missing—people often will lack drive.

It's important for moving forward and for the creative process that people perceive a void in their life. The emptiness creates the driving force and the creative force of innovation. When individuals become truly frustrated with their circumstances and they know life can be better, creative forces enter the mind and innovation is born. Most of life's comforts and enhancements were born out of frustration with what is and the desire to have something better and different.

1

When you're content and successful, that can be the ceiling for you. But when you have a feeling of discontentment and a perception that you're unsuccessful, the driving force to make a change and to create a better life is born. From birth, our inabilities and discontentment assist us in our milestones. For a baby, the frustration of being immobile creates the desire for movement. For a young child, the frustration of not being comprehended creates the mastery of language. Whatever you perceive is missing in your life, you wish to have.

When a person is sick and has ill health or injuries, health and physical vitality become a priority of high value. When a person perceives himself or herself to be dumb or ill informed, mental empowerment becomes a high value. The man or woman with a perception of social isolation desires friendships and social networks. The person without a family or a couple without children often develop the desire for a family and having a family becomes a high priority. People without a vision and a life purpose seek meaning in their lives. When it's time to choose a career or a vocation, the search for service and finding a vocational purpose becomes of high importance. The search for money and the absence of money can become a strong driving force and a high priority for the man or woman who perceives lack of wealth as creating pain, suffering, challenges, and feeling unsuccessful.

Whatever you perceive is most missing in your life becomes that *one thing* you seek. Whatever you're seeking, you're willing to spend your time on it without hesitation, and nobody has to remind you to attend to it. You're thinking about it a lot and it dominates your thoughts. What becomes important to you, you wish to read about and learn about, and you have a hunger for knowledge about that topic. Anything you're curious about and desire to know more about will prompt you to put in the time, energy, focus, and dedication to learn about it. You'll have the intrinsic motivation to equip yourself with wisdom and knowledge on that subject. Just by watching what a person reads or searches for on the Internet, you can get a strong indication of what the most important priorities are for that person.

Perceiving a Lack of Money and What That Can Ignite

I've heard many people's stories over the years and I've read enough biographies, books, and articles about successful and financially empowered people to know that most of the time, a perception of lack and void is the innovating trigger for wealth creation.

A family who consulted with me shared their family story, and it echoes many other stories with similar narratives. The first generation (man or woman) moved at a very young age from one country, which at the time of exit was in a financially disempowered state, to a country with better prospects. Some of these émigrés are as young as fourteen years old. The young man or woman arrives in a foreign country—the proverbial promised land—with very little money, education, or possessions. The individual narrative will be different after arrival, but typically the story goes like this: They start working as blue-collar laborers, learn to speak the language, and start to make an income. This humble beginning—and the dire need for money for pure survival—ignites in the man or woman the extraordinary character traits of survival, self-growth, entrepreneurship, innovation, creativity, and perseverance.

The first generation—with the high focus, attention, time intensity, high drive, and dedication to fill an empty wallet—develops a highly concentrated and narrow focus on wealth creation. The struggle leads to the development of character, determination, the willingness to work hard, and perseverance. Many of them become larger-than-life figures. It's understandable that when a void gets filled and what has been missing is provided, the idea of ownership is an easy next step for the person creating the wealth. It's undeniable that what you perceive to be your highest, most important priority becomes your identity and your destiny in life. It's inevitable that your focus, intention, attention, intrinsic motivation, time intensity, and inspiration become part of who you are, defining your identity, what your life demonstrates, and what you're known for.

What are the most important mindsets and life-long habits that these individuals develop when they focus their intention on creating wealth—first of all, narcissistically, for improving their own lives and second, altruistically, for improving the lives of their family? These mindsets and habits are recommended for every generation. Just as money can grow like a snowball in a family, the same is true for mindsets and habits. They can also grow like snowballs in a family until the mindsets and habits become part of the family's DNA.

They Have a Vision for Their Family's Wealth Creation

They know that the secret to creating and growing wealth for their family is to have a big enough reason to want to do it. The desire to grow and create wealth to buy more things is not a good enough reason, although wealth does make it possible to buy more things. A bigger reason makes it more worthwhile. They chose to create and grow wealth for their family to give them the best as well as to make the world a better place. Imagine how fulfilling it would be if you, like Bill and Melinda Gates through their foundation, focused on increasing health conditions worldwide. In *Family Wealth,* James Hughes says, "A family can successfully preserve wealth for more than one hundred years if the family governance and practices are founded on shared values that express the family's differentness." This can only be done if someone is creating and holding the vision for the family—a vision for at least a hundred years.

They Adapt the Best Strategy and Priorities to Create and Grow Their Family Wealth

Whenever I ask a group of people, "Who wants to be financially independent?" most people put up their hands. The reality is that less than 1 percent will become financially independent. To enable you to be true to your heart's desire to create and grow wealth for your family, you need to develop the right strategy, mindset, and priorities to do it.

Set your attention on it, spend your energy on it, read and learn about it, talk about it, think about it, and be inspired about it. Learn to create and grow wealth through great service delivery and a strategic building up of wealth. Forget about quick fixes and overnight success. Strategies build wealth.

They Adapt the Eighth Wonder of the World

Albert Einstein referred to compound interest as the eighth wonder of the world. They understand the eighth wonder and know their money grows, even while they're sleeping. They develop the healthy habit of saving. Saving is another way to look at paying yourself first. The wealthiest people in the world keep a big portion of their wealth portfolio liquid, another form of saving. The more you save, the more money flows to you, because money goes where it is appreciated. Your emotions, thoughts, and feelings about your wealth will be less volatile the more you save, as your savings acts as your cushion.

They Learn to Manage Their Emotions about Money

Warren Buffett is famous for his wealth accumulation and for saying, "Until you learn to manage your emotions about wealth, you will not get more money to manage." Feelings of guilt, fear, shame, and uncertainty are not the feelings of a wealth creator for the family. Instead, they develop the skill to make swift decisions with certainty and listen to their own genius inner voice. They learn life skills to manage their emotions.

They Value Teaching Their Children Good Money Habits

They start when the children are young and make it their focus and aim to teach them good money habits. They know children learn the most by watching them. They neither spoil them nor become a scrooge. I have to add that the most powerful families that build generational wealth for the benefit of the family and society start with educating their children when they're very young. Many first-generation parents who create wealth, however, do not focus on financially educating their children, and they often raise financially disempowered children. For these families, the proverb is waiting to come true.

They Understand the Importance of Husband and Wife Teamwork

The axiom "Behind every great man there's a great woman" indicates that one's chances of success increase if one has a great partner. A study by Brittany C. Solomon and Joshua J. Jackson of Washington University in St. Louis shows that "having a conscientious spouse can boost your income." Such couples know that the more closely they're aligned and working as a team, with the same goals, vision, and dreams for the family, the more successful they'll be in creating and growing the family wealth. The wealth creation is not the *job* of one person. They understand it's a joint effort of supporting each other and delegating tasks and functions to each other to make the "business called their family" more streamlined.

They Develop the Habit of Delayed Gratification

We live in a time of immediate gratification—having what we want without delay. Until you make peace with the habit of delayed gratification, you'll prefer spending your hard-earned money rather than growing it. The wise wealth creators save their money until they have at least three to six months of income saved, then they study investment options and start to invest. By offering a great service or product, earning money through fair exchange, saving, and investing money, they steadily grow and increase the wealth they're building for their family. They have a long-term vision and take the steps toward it daily, and they do it with delayed gratification as their mantra. They don't compare themselves with the Joneses. Rather, they compare themselves to their own goals, dreams, and vision.

The Power of Knowing What's Most Important to You

You can waste your time, energy, and focus if you allow someone else's priorities to obscure your own authentic priorities and what is most important to you. This is one of the dangers rising generations face, meaning all the generations following the first generation of the family. The larger-than-life first generation can come across as so successful, so certain, so overpowering, and so prescriptive that their dominance can lead to the projection of first-generation priorities onto following generations. It's the birthright of every person to live his or her dreams, hopes, wishes, goals, and vision—not someone else's.

In his book *The Voice of the Rising Generation,* James Hughes explains the rising generation as follow: "The rising generation is not simply young, or second or next. Most fundamentally, it is an attitude or a state of mind. A rising generation is defined not by biology or finances but by psychology. The core element of this psychology is an awareness of growth, possibility and hope. As a member of the rising generation you recognize that you are far from finished. You may have barely begun." As the first generation has clearly identified and lived their lives according to what is of highest importance to them, so it is the birthright of every following generation.

How Do You Know What Is of Highest Importance and Priority to You — And Why Is It Important to Know?

Socrates said, "A tethered specimen is very valuable for they are magnificent creations. And that, I must say, has a bearing on the matter of true opinions. True opinions are a fine thing and do all sorts of good as long as they stay in their place, but they will not stay long. They run away from a man's mind, so they are not worth much until you tether them by working out the reason. Once they are tied down, they become knowledge and they become stable."

As long as you look at life from a perception of lower value and uncertainty about your role, purpose, contribution, and uniqueness, you will live life according to the voices from the outside and those in your life whom you perceive to have the most certainty. Your uncertainty about what you value as highly important for yourself will be overshadowed by the more certain opinions of others. If you look up to your first generation as the powerful and certain ones, the captain of your ship, that focus can have the devastating effect of minimizing your own drives, and you can then easily confuse what you perceive they want from you as what is truly important for you. The biggest gift a man or a woman can give himself or herself is to know with certainty what is of highest personal value, importance, and priority.

What are the signs that you're living your life according to what is of highest importance and priority to you?

- **You use words that affirm what's important to you.** You use words that affirm you *love* doing what you're doing, you're *inspired* by what you're doing, you feel it's your *destiny* to do it, and you *choose* and *live* to do it.
- **Your life shows with certainty what is of highest importance and priority to you.** That's because you dedicate your life to the actions, focus, and achievement of what is of highest importance and priority to you. You continuously think about what is important to you. You love to talk about what is important to you and you direct conversation to the topic and themes you value as most important to you. You wake up and become animated, and your self-confidence and self-esteem strengthen when you're focused on your highest values and highest priorities.

Dr. John Demartini, human behavior specialist and polymath, writes in his book *The Values Factor:* "Knowing your highest values vastly increases your patience and perseverance. When you seek to achieve a goal that aligns with your highest values, you increase your patience, integrity, and leadership."

You can ask yourself high-quality questions to help clarify what is of highest value, importance, and priority to you. I believe the following compilation of questions by Dr. John Demartini is concise and revealing. Answer each one with at least three items and make sure they're authentically your answers and not merely how you wish things to be. If you answer with items representing your *wishes rather than reality*, you're not going to determine your true authentic values, high priorities, and what's truly of importance to you.

Demartini Value Determination Questions

1. How do you fill your personal and/or professional space?
2. How do you spend your time?
3. How do you spend your energy and when you do it, it energizes you?
4. How do you spend your money?
5. Where do you have the most order and organization?
6. Where are you most reliable, disciplined, and focused?
7. What do you think about, and what are your innermost dominant thoughts? Exclude negative thoughts.
8. What do you visualize and realize?
9. What is your internal dialogue? Exclude negative self-talk.
10. What do you talk about in social settings?
11. What inspires you?
12. What are the most consistent long-term goals you have set?
13. What do you love to learn and read most about?

Once you've answered all thirteen questions with three items per question, you'll have thirty-nine listed items. Notice the repetition in the listed answers and find the answer you've repeated the most, then the answer you repeated the second most, then the answer you repeated the third most. By counting the answers you've repeated, you'll be able to determine which answer appeared as most important, second important, and third important. This way you can determine your highest values, top priorities, and what is most important to you.

Here is an example of a hypothesis of the answers and highest values, top priorities, and what is most important to a successful and authentic, true-to-him-or-herself rising generation with a heart for growing and preserving the family wealth:

1. How do you fill your personal and/or professional space?
   - Books on self-development and self-empowerment

- Business and financial magazines and newspapers
- Computer used for research on trends and patterns in the marketplace

2. How do you spend your time?

- Reading books on self-development and self-empowerment, business, as well as financial magazines and newspapers
- Working in the family business
- Socializing with friends

3. How do you spend your energy?

- Exercising in the gym
- Working in the family business
- Reading

4. How do you spend your money?

- Saving and investing
- Books, magazines, and newspapers
- Lifestyle

5. Where do you have the most order and organization?

- My reading material
- My work schedule
- My social calendar

6. Where are you most reliable, disciplined, and focused?

- At work
- My reading and research
- Exercises

7. What do you think about, and what are your innermost dominant thoughts?

- How do I grow the family business in my own vision?
- How do I grow my own finances and become successful in my own right?
- Who will be my ideal life partner?

8. What do you visualize and realize?
   - Expanding the family business globally
   - Finding the ideal life partner
   - Growing my own finances

9. What is your internal dialogue?
   - How do I grow the family business to be on all the continents?
   - What is happening in the financial world?
   - What do I want in the ideal life partner?

10. What do you talk about in social settings?
    - What I learn in the books, magazines, and newspapers I'm reading
    - Business and what is happening in the financial world
    - My family

11. What inspires you?
    - Successful families
    - Successful entrepreneurs
    - Visionaries

12. What are the most consistent long-term goals that you have set?
    - Making my mark in the business world
    - Growing my own wealth
    - Having a successful and fulfilling marriage and family of my own

13. What do you love to learn most about?
    - Business
    - Finance
    - Self-empowerment

When you count the items most frequently repeated—from first to sixth—you'll see the following hierarchy of values, priorities, and high importance:

1. Business
2. Finances

3. Self-development
4. Family
5. Social
6. Exercise

What this hierarchy means is the following: this person is dedicated and is assigning high value, importance, and priority to the items on the list as mentioned. That is a high indicator of success for this person, because whatever you focus on, dedicate yourself to, fill your mind with, spend your time on, and set your goals for, that is where success appears. It's one of the most important pieces of information and insight in understanding and knowing yourself—knowing your hierarchy of values, priorities, and what is truly important to you. This is your authentic self and your true self. "Know yourself, be yourself, love yourself," said the Oracle of Delphi.

Live Your Destiny and Leave Your Mark

"There are [people], who by their sympathetic attraction carry nations with them and lead the activity of the human race."
~Ralph Waldo Emerson

Every person who has ever been born and those still to be born has a reason, purpose, mission, and destiny. It does not matter the family you're born in or the vision your parents have for you. What matters is what you wish to do with your life. What is of utmost importance for you is to know what you consider most important and what you want to be known for. When you have no idea what's most important to you, you can feel overwhelmed—filled with anxiety, insecurity, and uncertainty. Fortunately, this information is not hidden from you. Your life, your actions, your words, your language, your choices, and your decisions demonstrate it. It is showcased to the world.

Your hierarchy of values—what you perceive to be of highest importance and priority for you—is your purpose and ultimately your destiny. What you perceive to be missing in your life becomes most important to you; therefore, you can confirm the words of Clarissa Judd, director of the Demartini Institute and a master Demartini Method facilitator: "Voids become high values and translate into life wealth."

There is a proverb, with variations around the world, that says families go from "shirtsleeves-to-shirtsleeves in three generations." Being born in a family with financial means can distract you from the desire to create wealth, since you don't perceive any void in wealth or financial means. Being born into family wealth creates a unique set of voids, and every next generation has to face the challenge of being born with the so-called "golden spoon in your mouth." This advantage can create the false illusion that money comes easily, and entitlement and a lack of self-achievement and self-preservation can develop. Unless the rising generation develops a clear sense of self with their own unique vision and mission for their lives, the shirtsleeves proverb might very likely become true for the family.

Because the first generation perceived a void relating to money, creating money to keep the wolves at bay became their vision, mission, and destiny. The same must be true for every generation that follows. The difference is that for the succeeding generations, the void is not a lack of money and finances. They're born into a family with wealth and financial means. But for every individual born in a family with financial means, a different void develops. Every person makes decisions about how he or she perceives life, and every perception is made based on lopsided perceptions. No point of view or perception is based on an ultimate truth. Every point of view or perception is made using the lenses through which the person views life. This perception acts as a truth for the observer, but with artful human behavior skills and high-quality questions, any perception can be changed. Therefore, every man and woman will form unique perceptions, through his or her own lenses.

Whatever you perceive is missing in your life will become a perception you wish to change. The bigger the desire to change what you perceive to be missing, the more it becomes your *telos,* or your purpose or destiny. Your life will also demonstrate what you wish to change because you'll make it a high priority of great importance to you. Just as the first generation wished to change their financial destiny, the following generations are wise to ask themselves what they wish to change in their lives and what action steps they're prepared to take to bring about the changes.

You were not born to build your parents' dreams. Neither were you born to build any other family member's dreams. You were born to make your own dreams come true and to build your own ideal life. Whatever you dream of making of your life, whatever your burning desires are, whatever you dedicate your life to fulfilling is your destiny and will become the mark you leave on the world. Ask the following question over and over until you get more certainty: What do I want to be known for? What do I wish to dedicate my life to?

From your biggest frustrations, innovation is born. Discontent with what is, your disappointments, and your distress awaken your creativity, goal-setting, and action steps that bring the changes you wish for. You know things could be and should be better, but you just don't know how to make them better. You decide to walk toward the problem, not dance around it, and you create your mission, vision, and purpose, and thereby your destiny. It's right in front of your eyes and has always been there, in your frustrations, your discontent. That's how your destiny is born. When you awaken the genius in you through your sheer discontent and you have a burning desire to make a change in your life, you take another step in the direction of your destiny and the mark you will leave with your uniqueness and extraordinary approach. Nobody has your voids, nobody has your perceptions, and nobody has your dreams and wishes to do or have things differently. They combine to make your unique and extraordinary contribution to the world, and only you can do it in the way you will do it.

Your perception of your disappointments, challenges, pain, losses, failures, and lack of success all become your driving force and the big bad wolf you wish to escape. Through your action steps, your decisions, your choices, and your attention and intention, you create that which is of highest importance, highest value, and highest priority to you, and that's how your purpose and destiny are formed. When the expectations on you to perform certain duties concerning the family wealth do not make your heart sing and are not your heart's desire, that is valuable feedback to you: it is not your thing.

People who desire to live an extraordinary life, authentic to what is of highest importance to them, develop the following habits:

- **They never ever give up.** They are "I can" people, saying "I unhook the *t* from *can't.*"
- **They find what they love to do**—and dedicate their life to it. It does not matter what it is, as long as it is what they love doing and it makes them tap dance through their days. Living a life with joy and meaning contributes to feeling purposeful and fulfilled.
- **They live with a vision and purpose.** Every person is born with a purpose and a reason for being. It's no secret what your purpose is, because your life, your actions, and your decisions reflect your purpose. Your purpose becomes more tangible as you translate it into a vision. No matter how big or small you perceive your vision to be, it is uniquely yours, and nobody can have the same vision as you. The world needs everyone's vision. Your vision comprises your acts of service to others and yourself.
- **They leave a legacy.** When you start to think about and plan the impact you wish to have, you can choose how far ahead you wish to think and plan. Whether you think small or big, its takes up the same time and space in your mind. What is the gift you wish to leave to your loved ones, your community, your country, and the world? What is the outreach of the purpose you wish to have? Why not think in terms of generations? The plans and thoughts take up the same time and space in your mind as a one-generation thinking.
- **They have a master plan for their life.** Plan how you wish your life to unfold in all areas. What about growing your spiritual awareness, your mental power, your vocational service, your financial prosperity, your caring family relationships, your social leadership and impact, and your physical health and vitality? How will your life look

when you're focused on being empowered and inspired in all the areas of your life?

There are three powerful steps to master planning your life:

1. Have a burning desire for your life.
2. Take definite action steps to achieve your burning desire.
3. Develop an attitude of gratitude. The more you count your blessings, the more blessings you will get to count.

You are here for your reason, your destiny, your life, and your dreams. Know them. Live them. Be them. Give yourself permission to be authentic and true to yourself. By doing this, the snowball of perpetual motion of visionaries, visions, destinies, and legacies will be built for your family. The purpose of family wealth then takes on a much bigger form. It is the right of every family member and every generation to live fulfilled, prosperous, meaningful, and impactful lives. Nobody is born to live someone else's life, dreams, or vision. Living your own authentic life will break the shirtsleeves-to-shirtsleeves in three generations proverb in your family. Hence, the biggest contribution you can make toward building your multigenerational family—where every member in every generation has the privilege to a fulfilled, meaningful, and purposeful life—*is to live a fulfilled, meaningful, and purposeful life.*

CHAPTER 2

The Wealth Creator Extraordinaire

It is my wish for you to have a deep understanding of what it means to have a mission, vision, and purpose for your life. Every person ever born and every person who has lived on planet Earth has a unique mission, vision, and purpose. Unfortunately, not everyone is aware of that unique mission, vision, and purpose and therefore lives the dreams and vision of those they perceive as more empowered. My wish for everyone reading this book is that you'll become aware of and inspired by your own unique mission, vision, and purpose and that you therefore will live your life with meaning, fulfillment, and inspiration. Everyone has the birthright of uniqueness and purposefulness. If you don't have certainty of your dreams and you don't build your own dreams, you will end up building someone else's dreams.

It's the dream and desire of most parents that their children continue to build on the dreams and desires they gave birth to, whether it's the family business, a collection of businesses, a property, or a vast fortune. It is, however, the right of every child of these parents to live their own dreams, desires, goals, and visions. It is, therefore, the responsibility of every person and that means you, to gain certainty about what you wish for your life and what goals you wish to set to achieve your wishes.

My life would have been very different and I would have lived a life building someone else's dreams if I had not been introduced to the mindset, human behavior, and action steps to live my meaningful, purposeful, and inspiring life. My heart's desire is to share with you what I've discovered by studying the great minds in history. Little of what I share with you is my original thinking or discovery, but every man and woman who made a mark in history and who lived—and still are living—meaningful, purposeful, and inspiring lives had access to these universal truths and insights. Rather than inventing a new wheel, I learned from the great minds that graciously shared about purpose, meaning, vision, mission, and fulfillment.

The Greek philosopher Aristotle said that man's purpose is to pursue happiness. I believe what creates one's happiness is being in a state of gratitude and love, and that these states will be in moments not in life's entirety. The wish for happiness and, therefore, the wish for gratitude and love can only be realistically attained as we accept that they happen in moments. Otherwise, we create fantasies in our minds, which lead to nightmares in our lives. Love and gratitude happen in moments of grace.

In this chapter, I wish to share with you how to predict your destiny by creating it. This superb suggestion was made by Albert Einstein, the scientist and philosopher. I wish to inspire you to own the immense value you offer to the world by owning your purpose, mission, and vision. And finally, I wish for you to own your meaning and your fulfillment by the unique and individualized way you live your life.

You are valuable to the world.

Live with a Vision and a Mission

A person who lives with a vision and a mission is inspiring to be with. When you live with an awareness of your vision and mission, you also feel more inspired to be with yourself. Empowered individuals strive to live a life of meaning, inspiration, fulfillment, and purpose, and that makes them some of the most extraordinary people on the planet. Most people wish to be someone different and extraordinary, and I'm certain that you have it in you to be that extraordinary person. I've heard countless times, "I don't have a vision and mission," and each time I've heard it, I've said, "Everyone has a vision and a mission." The difference between those who have awareness of their vision and mission and those who don't is this: those who know their vision have awareness and have taken action steps to clarify and define their vision and mission. When you live your life with meaning, inspiration, fulfillment, and purpose, your time and space horizon expand and you feel that your effort and hard work are worthy and impactful. Psychiatrist and Holocaust survivor Viktor Frankl said, "He who has a *why* to live can bear with almost any *how*."

The bigger the *why* you want to live a life of meaning, the more readily you will find the *how* to make your life meaningful. To those with purpose and a dedicated life plan to unfold and realize their dreams and hopes, the journey of life becomes an adventure.

Meaning and Purpose

Nobody can give you a meaning and purpose in life. Each of us has free choice to decide what we want to dedicate our lives to. The wealth creator extraordinaire decides on a definite purpose and high-priority action steps and action plans to live out their purpose. The bigger you plan to live your life, the bigger meaning your dreams will have and the more likely your desires will become burning desires that will guide and lead you to live an extraordinary life and take action to fulfill the desires of your heart. Whether you dream big or dream small, it takes the same time and space in your mind.

You might feel you have no idea what your dreams are or what you want to dedicate your life to. You might be one of the many men and women who have an inkling of what you want your life to be about, but you don't have enough intrinsic motivation to take the action steps to achieve your dreams. Everyone knows what they want, but not everyone give themselves the permission to live their life they way they wish. The first step is to give yourself permission to live your life the way you wish to live it, not in a narcissistic way, without a care for anyone, but rather, in a caring way, where you give yourself and others the permission and freedom to live authentic, meaningful lives.

Legacy and Meaning

Some people dream for tomorrow, others for next year, others for the next decade, and others, the extraordinary ones, dream for generations. They dream of legacies and impact and meaning and making a difference—not because they have such big egos that they can't live without adoration and applause from others but because they know they have a purpose and a reason for being alive. Their lives are not just a random act; there is a specific, purposeful reason they're alive. They don't have the answer to the *why;* they dedicate their lives to finding out. And in their dedication to finding the answers, life becomes meaningful and important.

Living a life dedicated to the legacy you wish to leave expands your sphere of awareness as well as your sphere of influence. There are many choices in life. There is the choice to live your life by making an impact on your family, or your community, or your neighborhood, or your city, or your province, or your country, or your continent, or the world, or the universe, or the galaxy. You get to decide how big a legacy you wish to leave and for how many years. It can be from one day to a thousand years. It's all about your intention and your wish for meaning, impact, and influence. If your legacy is about self-aggrandizement, your intention is narcissistic and self-centered and your success will be short lived. If your legacy is about your life purpose, vision, and mission, success increases dramatically.

Leaving a legacy can sound overwhelming and out of your league. But every person has the choice to think bigger than today and live for a bigger reason. The oldest family firm, Takenaka Corporation, has been in existence since 1610. In 1610, Tobei Masataka Takenaka, a shrine and temple carpenter, started a business in Nagoya, Japan. The business was run as a family business and built some of the first Western-style buildings during the last half of the nineteenth century, most of them in Nagoya. In 1899, Toemon Takenaka, a fourteenth-generation descendant of the original founder, established a branch office in Kobe, Japan, and founded Takenaka Corporation as an official company.

This family business's legacy has lasted hundreds of years. The only way a family business can remain in the family for multiple generations, as in the case of the Takenaka Corporation, is because of the legacy, vision, and mission of the family. By family, we don't mean every family member. We mean the dedication, vision, mission, and legacy of the family leader of each generation.

The wealth creator extraordinaire creates and dreams of a legacy for the family beyond his or her own lifetime. Wealth creators think and plan and hold the vision for their family as an act of love and care. They know it starts with a thought, because thoughts become things, as Albert Einstein famously remarked. For anything to be birthed, there must be a conceiver. A legacy is conceived by a man or a woman in the family with the most certainty and a big enough *why*. By giving life to the creation of a legacy, energy transforms into matter and a physical manifestation is brought to life. Until a legacy is created as a vision and a mission for a family, the legacy is formless and the energy and potential of the family remain unmanifested.

Creating and manifesting a legacy for your family into material existence generates meaning for your family. A family with meaning, vision, and mission has a bigger sphere of awareness and influence than a family without it. The bigger the vision, mission, and burning desire you have for the continuation of your family in perpetuity, the bigger the chance of manifesting your desire. It all starts with a dream, a burning desire; that is the seed, the fertilization of the manifestation of your powerful generational family for the ultimate fulfillment, prosperity, and inspiration of each family member in perpetuity. *True authentic wealth creation is a lifelong, dedicated, action-driven journey toward reaching your heart's desire to create wealth for a higher purpose.*

Vision, Mission, Dream, and Legacy—Building Your Powerful Family

Purpose of the Vision, Keeper of the Dream

Happiness is not a state of being. It is a result of choices, options, and mindsets. Our highest calling is the pursuit of *fulfillment* and *prosperity* in all areas of our lives—namely spiritual, mental, vocational, financial, familial, social, and physical. A truly powerful family is a family dedicated to unlocking the high net worth, or highest potential, in each individual member of the family, with the purpose of building a powerful family for generations to come, enabling the ultimate fulfillment and prosperity of each member as well as for the collective family.

No family is bonded only by blood relationships; the stronger bonding is by affinity. *Affinity* refers to a natural liking or attraction to a person. It goes beyond blood relationships, and according to James Hughes in *Family Wealth,* it includes all family relationships that "are defined by their openness to fostering individual dreams and growth; in so doing, they offer fertile possibilities for the successful undertaking of each family member's most important work." The more freedom every individual in the family has to develop and pursue personal fulfillment and prosperity within the bonds of affinity—and with insight into the family legacy—the more the individual and family develop richly for generations to come.

A family starts with two people coming together with the intention to stay together in a partnership for life. I have yet to meet a couple, whether heterosexual or homosexual, who did not have the intention and hope that the relationship would last. Most people like to believe in the fantasy "and they lived happily together forever and ever." From the two, the family starts, and once children come along, it's called a family.

I believe every family has a reason, or purpose, for coming together. Energetically, there is a higher purpose and higher reason for family members coming together as a collective. That purpose is oftentimes born from either of the starting couple or from both.

Every well-managed family should have a vision and mission statement. The vision of the family, together with their mission statement, defines the family as unique and it binds the members of the family together with bonds of affinity. The visionary of the family, the one holding the long-term purpose and reason for the family, will create the family vision. The visionary may be the father or the mother or both. It is the person or persons whose highest value is to create and hold the vision for the family. A vision cannot be forced or created out of selfish needs. A vision is going to be as successful as each individual member perceiving their highest fulfillment and prosperity. The unlocking of their potential will result from the vision.

In creating the family vision and holding the vision for generations to come, the following elements contribute to successfully defining it:

1. An authentic vision is heartfelt and written with the intention that it serves every family member for generations to come. It's not intended to control or to subscribe to anyone.
2. An authentic vision has the unlocking of each family member's potential as a high value and priority.
3. An authentic vision has a large time horizon, and its architecture enhances the bonds of affinity among the family members for multiple generations. It holds a big picture for the family, as far as seven generations. Imagine you're the creator of a vision for your family that will affect your descendants for multiple generations and your dream and vision you're holding for your family is felt 300 years later.
4. An authentic vision includes all the areas of life, not only the areas the visionary might deem important. Human behavior experts and psychologists offer the following approach to covering all areas of life. In Western societies, it's referred to as *the wheel of life*.

The wheel of life consists of the following components: spiritual mission, mental wisdom, vocational or career fulfillment, financial management, family relationships, social relationships and impact, and lastly, physical health and vitality. Every person encounters all areas of the wheel of life, from birth to death. According to the developmental stage of life and values, some areas in the wheel of life will be of more interest and importance to that person and others will be of less importance. A truly powerful family has as part of their vision: empowerment, unlocking of potential, fulfillment, and prosperity in all the areas on the wheel of their life.

The empowered and authentic wealth creator extraordinaire is a man or a woman with a vision, mission, dream, and legacy to build a powerful family in more areas than just wealth in the sense of finances. They also have the vision, mission, dream, and legacy to build a powerful family in all areas of life. They know that money is just the means to a vision and mission, and the focus on empowerment in all areas of life is the more authentic way to live with fulfillment and meaning. They're big-picture thinkers and they think out of the box. They don't favor comfort zones. They love to dream with realism because life is too exciting and meaningful to miss out on what is the potential of every family and every family member. They say they can *and they do*.

They see a picture of their family beyond what anyone else can see and they hold that picture with certainty, conviction, faith, and trust. They see their powerful family as a family with a legacy, vision, mission, and purpose, and they dedicate their dreams and vision to creating a family that's empowered in all areas of life. All areas of life can be referred to as the areas that form the spikes of a wheel, namely:

1. **Spiritual vision and mission.** Everyone has a spiritual vision and mission. It's the reason you're alive. It's the reason your soul came into a physical body. It's your meaning and your purpose, and it's unique to you. Nobody has or will ever have your form of vision and mission and the world needs it at the time of your existence.

2. **Mental genius.** Everyone is a mental genius in the areas of their dedication and what they believe is of highest importance. Your perceived voids and pains are constantly feeding your mental genius. You wish to learn and empower yourself in the very areas you perceive you're the most lost or behind. You want to learn about aspects in your life where you perceive you're overpowered and where you feel stupid or dumb. Striving for mental mind mastery is one of the biggest gifts you can give yourself. To have it as a priority to consistently work toward mental mastery is a lifelong job with lifelong benefits and gains. The more you learn to master your mind, the more you learn to master your life.

3. **Vocational service.** Everyone is born with a heart for service to others and to himself. It's therefore the responsibility of everyone to find out what he or she loves to do and loves to offer as a service. It creates meaning and fulfillment to be of service and to make a difference in the lives of others and yourself. It does not mean your offer of service has to be a service for material gain. It can be a service to your family, like the full-time mother, or service to society, like the philanthropist. It's equally the student who takes his or her studies and schoolwork seriously and makes it a goal to do his or her best to use and expand their gifts, talents, and uniqueness.

4. **Financial intelligence.** Everyone has the choice and option to develop his or her financial intelligence and genius. You do not necessary have to become a banker, financial advisor, auditor, or accountant. Financial intelligence refers to the ability to understand, study, read, and research finances. It refers to your understanding of the universal principle of fair exchange. Fair exchange refers to the protocol whereby parties agree to deliver an item if and only if they receive an item or service in return. Financial intelligence also understands the wisdom of saving and investing and the wonder of compound interest. A financially intelligent person also understands the wisdom of emotional intelligence in the support and alignment of financial intelligence.

They understand the wisdom of emotional self-control in the management of money and that money with a purpose is money with meaning. A meaningful life is a life supported by meaningful finances, where finances are used for lifestyle and for far more than lifestyle. A meaningful life is a life in which finances are used to create meaning and service to mankind for uplifting men, women, and children. It's far bigger than the accumulation of material possessions and experiences. It's about making a difference.

5. **Family relationships.** Everybody comes from a family, and belonging to a meaningful and caring family is among a person's most important needs. A successful family has a fundamental interest in others' well-being and the greater understanding of others and self. Successful families have individuals with the mindset and heart of caring about other people and caring for themselves. They balance caring for others and the self, for the ultimate enhancement and development of each one involved. A family that consists of family members who care has the greatest potential to be successful. Because we all have a deep inner drive to be of purpose and meaning and to make a difference, the roadmap to a successful family must be nested in the acts of service to others.

Because each family consists of many family members, both through blood bonds and bonds of affinity, each family consists of a multitude of talents, abilities, skills, and acts of service. A successful, caring family creates the opportunity for everyone in the family to live their lives in true alignment with what is of importance, value, and priority to them. A successful family is created when everyone in the family does what they love and love what they do and when the family structure and wealth (both human potential and financial wealth) make it possible for everyone to be of service to others in the form they love for being of service.

I offer the following questions to help as a roadmap to building a successful family:

- Is everyone experiencing the freedom to follow dreams and goals?
- Is the family's human potential and financial capital encouraging the development and expression of uniqueness and individuation?
- Does every family member perceive his or her value and importance in the family?
- Does every family member have the opportunity and access to mentorship and receiving wise counsel?
- Does every family member perceive that they have a voice?
- Does every family member have awareness of his or her big-heartedness?

If we think a successful family is the family with the most financial wealth, the most opportunities for an extraordinary lifestyle, and the most professional degrees, we're far removed from understanding the true characteristics of a successful family. A successful family is the family in which everyone has the biggest opportunity to develop to their highest potential and to be of service to others and to themselves. Ultimately, a successful family consists of meaningful, inspiring, fulfilled, purposeful, and prosperous family members.

If the most important structure of belonging is our association with a family, then the purpose of a family is to bring out the best in everyone in the family as well as everyone who comes into contact with the family, both directly and indirectly.

Successful family equals big-hearted individuals with service to others.

Social Networks and Leadership

Everyone is a leader, and your social leadership is in the area of your life you feel socially the most inspired by, most dedicated to, and most focused on. It is in the area in which you socially spend most of your time and energy, and where you're most ordered, organized, disciplined, and reliable. Don't let anyone tell you you're not a leader. Everyone is born a leader. The only difference between someone who takes on a leadership role and someone who doesn't is that the leader takes action and owns their form of leadership.

Your social leadership can come from being the family member who organizes most of the family get-togethers or the person who takes leadership in society. We need all forms of social leadership and the form you express it in is needed as much as any other form. There are many forms of social leadership to choose from; it can range from leadership in your family to leadership in your community, city, country, continent, or the world. The expression of your leadership will align with your highest priorities and importance. A mother taking leadership of her children's social events, organizing birthday parties, family Christmas dinners or lunches, family traditions like Bar Mitzvahs or coming-of-age celebrations plays a significant role in her family. She plays a significant role in the collecting and building of beautiful memories for family members and for the feeling of belonging in the family.

The social leader taking leadership of his friendship circle's social calendar—the one creating extraordinary experiences and taking responsibility to organize and arrange them all—is paying a significant role in building friendships, experiences, and bonding.

The person who takes leadership in his or her community and plays a role in enhancing and empowering the lives of the community is playing a significant and meaningful role in the community. So is the person who takes leadership in the enhancement and betterment of their city, country, or continent. The leadership role you choose to take on for the enhancement and improvement of mankind is your unique and extraordinary contribution to the world and will give you meaning, purpose, fulfillment, and inspiration.

One of the primal needs of every man, woman, and child is the need to belong. The need to belong to a family comes first and then follows the need to belong to a significant social group, circle, or network. The value of friendships is one of the significant ways you can feel meaning and purpose in your life. It's in the deeper and more significant connection with a person you call your friend that you give meaning to your life as well as to the life of your friends.

Friendships as an Enhancer of Life

Two are better than one; when the one falls down, the other can pick you up. One of the purposes of friendship is exactly this: to be there for each other. When you learn the art of meaningful and caring friendship relationships, you'll agree with me. It really enhances your life. Here are some guidelines in having a vision and mission for your friendships:

- Have certainty about the quality of the friendships you wish to form, nurture, and build. Know with certainty how you will describe your *ideal* (there is no such thing as an ideal friend; I use the word only as an indicator) and keep the seven areas of life in mind.
- Plan your action steps. In other words, what are you willing to do to attract the friends you wish to have in your life?
- Take action and build relationships. Explore what works for you and what does not work for you in the building of relationships.
- Be deeply grateful for the friendships you have already and be the friend you wish to have.

The more grateful you are for your friends, the more friends you will get to be grateful for.

Create extraordinary moments for and with your friends. This does not mean you must spend a lot of money to create these moments. The value is in the quality and relationship contribution for you and your friends. Everybody wants to belong and belonging to a special circle of friends is priceless.

Physical Health and Vitality

Imagine building your powerful family with the vision consisting of family members—both through blood relations and through bonds of affinity—who each have an awareness of a spiritual vision and mission, own the skills of a mental genius, dedicating their lives to offering their unique vocational service, doing what they love and loving what they do, with financial intelligence, warm, caring family relationships, inspiring social networks, and leadership—all by using their physically healthy bodies filled with vitality. What if you dedicated your vision for your family to incorporate all the mentioned spikes of the wheel? What family will your vision make possible? "What greater aspiration and challenge are there for a mother than the hope of raising a great son or daughter?" said Rose Kennedy.

Have a vision for the health of your body and of your mind. A healthy mind hosts a healthy body and a healthy body hosts a healthy mind. The two parts of you, namely your body and your mind, work hand in hand. They are interconnected and intertwined. You'll give yourself a great gift by having a vision and mission for your health, both mentally and physically.

Without the awareness that you can have a dream or a vision and mission for your health, you may live like many people do, with little connection and awareness of the gift of physical and mental health. I consider our bodies as the vehicle for taking our loving service to our loved ones, our friends, our community, the world, and to ourselves.

Consider the value and benefits of looking after your physical body. Consider with care and respect for yourself how you can look after your body, keeping the following in mind:

- Your diet, or way of eating
- Exercises, or the way you move and train your body
- Amount of water you drink
- Quality of your sleep
- The way you dress and groom yourself

Questions to Bring More Certainty about Your Vision, Mission, and Purpose

Author and motivational speaker Jack Canfield said, "I believe each of us is born with a life purpose and identifying, acknowledging, and honoring this purpose is possibly the most important action successful people take. They take the time to understand what they're here to do—and then they pursue that with passion and enthusiasm." The equally inspiring speaker and author Brian Tracy tells us, "Decide upon your major definite purpose in life and then organize all your activities around it."

Dr. John Demartini's approach to determining and connecting to your vision, mission, and purpose has been meaningful and impactful for me. I wish to share his approach with you.

- **Ask yourself high-quality questions.** The most important high-quality question is *Who do you want to be?* This question does not mean you must compare yourself to another person and say who you want to be in comparison. It means determining what you wish to be in all seven areas of life. As Einstein said, "Envy is ignorance and imitation is suicide."
- **Write down your own personal life purpose statement.** Here's an example:
  - My life purpose is to raise my children as world leaders.
  - My life purpose is to inspire and empower people to achieve their destiny.
  - My life purpose is to leave the world a better place for animals than I found it.
  - My life purpose is to provide employment for people through businesses.

"It's the soul's duty to be loyal to its own desires. It must abandon itself to its master passion," said British journalist Dame Rebecca West. When you live your life inspired each day because you live life taking your loving service to the world in your own unique way—demonstrated by *your value system, your words and actions, your enthusiasm,* and *your dreams*—you cannot wait to get up in the morning and you live in gratitude for your life, regardless of pain or pleasure, benefits or drawbacks, negatives, or positives. Author and public speaker Michael J. Gelb tells us, "Brain researchers estimate that your unconscious database outweighs the conscious data on an order exceeding ten million to one. This database is the source of your hidden, natural genius. In other words, a part of you is much smarter than you are. The wise people regularly consult that smarter part."

CHAPTER 3

The Genius of the Wealth Creator Extraordinaire

A genius is a person whose mind can be described with the following adjectives: brilliance, intelligence, ability, cleverness, wisdom, strength, and mastery. We all have a choice of how to use the power of our mind. We can either use our mind carelessly and without much thought, which most likely will make us behave like a fool. Or we can use our mind with care and tap into the mental genius, or leadership, that's available to all who strive for it. It takes dedication, hard work, and awareness of the power of the mind to actually tap into the mind's amazing power. We can stand on the shoulders of many mental genius giants to learn about the action steps to tap into the power of our minds. The more we educate ourselves about the power of our minds, the more we can tap into that power.

A truly powerful family develops a collective mindset of striving to mental mastery instead of mental slavery. There is collectively a treasure chest of wisdom present in families, and a mentally powerful family has a vision and a mindset of developing self-governance and self-mastery as a life task. Self-mastery is not a life task that can ever be achieved in a lifetime; rather, it's a journey, and every new generation starts the journey once again. Every new generation can have a head start if the previous generation is inspired and focused on sharing wisdom and mental intelligence. The more a family builds a wealth of mental intelligence as a source to tap into, the more the family members have the opportunity to develop their mental genius as a collective.

Traits of a Mentally Empowered, Intelligent Person

When one generation starts to own the traits of a mentally empowered and intelligent family, the snowball of mental genius and leadership is formed. A mentally empowered and intelligent family is created by the generation with the wisdom to focus on growing and developing a family with mentally empowered and intelligent family members for multiple generations.

This section looks at some of the traits of a mentally empowered and intelligent person.

Reflection and Transparency

"If we can see the greatness in others, it is because we can see it in ourselves," said Aristotle. People you interact with, whether for a brief moment or for a lifetime, act as your mirror and your reflection. Whatever you see in another person, you have in yourself, whether you see it or not. Every person has it all, but sadly, not every person knows it. The mentally empowered and intelligent person knows and applies the principle of "looking in the mirror," which is the principle of reflection and transparency: the mirror another human being is at any moment.

The generation who adopts the mindset of reflection and transparency is the generation who starts the mental empowerment state of mind for the family. Every person is a reflection of you. You have every trait that is listed in a dictionary and the uniqueness of that trait in you is your individualized expression of it. Every person has every trait and every person expresses all the traits uniquely according to their being and what is of highest importance, value, and priority to them. Because no two people have the same thumbprints, no two people express the human traits in the same way. When you see greatness in another person, it's a reflection of your greatness—your unique form of expression of the trait. The family with the mindset of owning human traits in their unique form of expression is a mentally brilliant family.

Humility

"If I have seen further, it is by standing on the shoulders of giants," Sir Isaac Newton confessed. Nobody knows it all and hubris, or excessive pride or self-confidence, is often the downfall of the person who perceives that he or she knows it all. An attitude of humility will take a person much further, because you open yourself up to being teachable, to learning from other people and tapping into the wisdom of people you consider role models and examples for you. Even the wise and clever scientist Sir Isaac Newton recognized the value of building on what others had done before.

Humility is described as the quality or state of not thinking you're better than other people—the quality or state of being humble. The more you humble yourself to learn from the wisdom of your first generation and people of previous generations as well as your own, the more you can empower your mind with the unique combination and interpretation of the information you gather. The mentally empowered person has an open mind and a teachable disposition.

Self-Reliance and Independence

"Strive in life to behave well," said American businessman and philanthropist Charlie Munger. The more a person develops the ability to be self-reliant and independent, the more the person has the ability and freedom to live his or her authentic life, with dedicated action steps toward his or her dream and goals. As long as you perceive yourself as dependent on others for your mental well-being and emotional ability to deal with life, you will stand in the way of your own growth.

Nobody can ever be fully independent, of course. It's a fantasy to strive for complete independence. As human beings, we need each other, and when we form relationships, we do form some dependency on the other person. I'm not encouraging a fantasy of total independence. I'm encouraging an independent mindset with the ability to behave well and handle the knocks of life in your own unique way, preferably with mental intelligence.

Knowledge of Human Behavior and Emotional Intelligence

An emotionally intelligent family has insight into human behavior, and their individual and joint goal is to know themselves and to know why people behave in the way they do. You don't need to become a psychologist to understand human behavior. Anyone can study human behavior, and anyone can develop the basic understanding that every person, no matter what age, stage, sex, or nationality, all act, react, decide, and behave 100 percent according to what they perceive to be of highest priority, importance, and value to them. Every man, woman, and child behaves the way they do because they perceive, whether consciously or subconsciously, that their behavior will give them more pleasure than pain, more positives than negatives, more gains than losses.

The driver and motivator for perceiving what is of high priority, high importance, and high value are found in the perception of loss—what a person perceives to be missing or lost in their lives becomes the driver and motivator that enables them to fill the void—the *missing*, the *lost*. Your perception of what is missing in your life will become the thing you value most. If you lack money, having money will become of high value, priority, and importance. If you lack health, having good health will become of high value, priority, and importance. If you lack friends, having friends will become of high value, priority, and importance. If you lack warm and caring relationships with family members, or your spouse, or your children, having warm and caring relationships with them will become of high value, priority, and importance to you. If you lack business success, having business success will become of high value, priority, and importance to you. If you perceive you have a mental void and you feel ignorant or unintelligent, having intelligence and knowledge will become of high value, priority, and importance to you. *Everybody behaves the way they do to fill perceived voids in their lives.*

When a husband/father or wife/mother lives in a way people describe as "workaholic," understanding their behavior means knowing they're doing it because they have a perception that something is missing, and becoming a workaholic is their attempt to fill the gap and bring meaning and purpose to their lives. Everybody does what he or she does out of the deep need to feel fulfilled, meaningful, prosperous, and inspired. Instead of blaming your father or mother for always working, change the way you look at their behavior and understand they're doing what they're doing to fill a void, something they perceive is missing.

Understand your own behavior and take note of the void or emptiness in your life. What is it you perceive as missing? What void are you trying to fill with your behavior? Nobody is on the planet to fulfill your needs and what you perceive to be missing in your life. You're responsible for the fulfillment of your own needs. You're responsible for discovering what is of importance, priority, and value for you, because these are the key ingredients of your life journey, assisting you to live your purpose, your destiny, your fulfilled life, your meaningful life, and your impact on the world.

Another component of understanding human behavior is to know that everyone lives their lives and behaves the way they do to secure the biggest advantage over their circumstances, the biggest support over challenge. The more we wish that a loved one, a business partner, a friend, a colleague, a neighbor, or even a stranger would change their behavior to make us happy and fulfill our needs, the more disillusioned and sad we become. We get entangled in a web of lopsided perceptions and unrealistic expectations and that leads to anger, bitterness, feeling challenged, despair and depression that looks for exits, and fatigue. An emotionally intelligent person understands that blaming, shaming, and accusations take you nowhere exciting. In fact, such behavior takes you down the dark hole of confusion, pain, sadness, resentment, and bitterness—a sad and lonely place.

Empower yourself with knowledge and insights about human behavior and invest in the way you use your mind. You can choose to use your mind by filtering your thoughts and perceptions and taking responsibility for your perceptions, or you can use your mind without any filters and allow lopsided perceptions and skewed opinions to control you. Powerful, inspiring, and impactful individuals use the power of their minds thoughtfully and caringly.

Mark Twain said, "Few things are harder to put up with than the annoyance of a good example." Choose to be an annoyance because of your lack of understanding of people's behavior or choose to be an annoyance because of your good example. You decide. You can *never* change another person. You can change only yourself. Taking responsibility is emotional intelligence. Acting with responsibility is emotional intelligence. Accepting others for who they are is called love.

Desire to Read and Learn

Mentally empowered people fill their minds with knowledge and information about their areas of interest as well as about world affairs. Every topic you can imagine has been written and spoken about. People who have a true hunger for knowledge and information realize it as a hunger that cannot be fully satisfied. To be the best torchbearer of the wealth perpetuation in your family for generations, develop the habit of reading and learning from those who studied and researched before you. Surround yourself with like-minded people, learn and study human behavior, business, finances, generational impact, leadership, self-mastery, philanthropy, physical health, and vitality. Learn about impact, influence, making a difference, having a meaning, living your life true to the hierarchy of your values and your telos (purpose). Learn and read about legacy, family relationships, the stock markets, philosophy, psychology, sociology, and theology and become a wealth of knowledge and information. Geniuses are people who become wise and apply their wisdom.

To become the torchbearer of your family's generational wealth and be one of the wealth builders for your family's generational perpetuity and impact, financially, business-wise, socially, family-wise, and physically (health and vitality), fill your mind with knowledge and wisdom and surround yourself with like-minded people. Learn from both those who lived before and those still alive.

Using affirmations, or words of power, can unlock your mental genius. Our words have power and can sentence us to life or death. Henry Ford said, "Whether you say you can or you say you can't, you are right." Geniuses place a muzzle in their mouth and filter their thoughts to control what words they speak aloud to others and silently to themselves.

Make a list of affirmations you would like to remind yourself of in unlocking your genius. Write them out, or type them and print the list and put it where you can see it often. Some people who drive a lot put the list on the steering wheels of their cars. Others put it on their bathroom mirrors or on the fridge in the kitchen. I have my mobile phone with me most of the time and I have beeps that go off at certain times during the day, reminding me of specific affirmations I want to remind myself of. Feed your mind with your endless possibilities and be the one who cultivates a fruitful mind as an example to others, now and for generations to come. You plant the mental seeds. Your generational impact is the soothing shade under which those following you can sit.

Understand and Apply Universal Principles

People who go through life without acknowledging universal laws or applying universal principles are people who journey through life blindfolded and cut off from the beautiful song of life itself. We're all living in a universe with the same principles for each and every one of us. Nobody is exempt from the laws of the universe. "Everywhere beneath the world's confusion there is an underlying order," said physicist Murray Gell-Mann.

Universal laws are the glue keeping everything together, and they're applicable to man, nature, and beast. Irrespective of your intelligence, your bank account, your health, your influence, or your life purpose, you're falling under the same universal laws as everyone else. Richard Feynman, considered by many to be Albert Einstein's successor, believed that if all scientific knowledge were destroyed and if only one statement could be passed on to the next generation, it should be the atomic hypothesis that "all things are made of atoms." He adds, "There is nothing that living things do that cannot be understood according to the laws of physics. All things are made of atoms, and everything that living things do can be understood in terms of the jigglings and wigglings of atoms."

To the man on the street, who may not have the brains of Einstein or Feynman, this simply means that because an atom is made of equal parts of positives and negatives and this phenomenon keeps the atom together, every experience that we as human beings experience has *atomic* components. That means every human experience has equal amounts of positives and negatives. The experience can only be because there are equal amounts of positives and negatives; otherwise, we would not be able to experience the event or feel the feelings or have the perceptions. This is a universal law.

We observe how there are opposites all around us; we notice how day changes into night, how summer is followed by winter, how we have tall and short people, old and young, happy and sad, challenges and support, pain and pleasure, waking and sleeping. The list is endless.

The moral of the story is everything has opposites; otherwise, we would not know that it exists. Everything has duality; everything has one side and an opposite side. Without duality we would not know, experience, or even exist! The smallest part of every human being is also an atom. So if an atom is equal parts positive and negative (duality), that means that every human being is also equal parts positive and negative (duality) and will therefore experience life as equally positive and negative.

The truth is that everything is in perfect balance and everybody will experience a perfect balance of:

- Pain and pleasure
- Drawbacks and benefits
- Negatives and positives
- Losses and gains
- Challenges and support
- Happiness and sadness
- Blessings and stressors

So from the field of physics we can draw these principles:

- All events in the universe are balanced events. So everything that happens to you is a balanced event, no matter whether it's pleasurable or painful.
- Every experience and every event has both positive and negative sides equally. Geniuses know that for everything negative, there is an equal and opposite positive.
- Energy is always conserved and nothing is ever missing. You are never without anything. It just might not exist in the form you wish.
- For every action there is an equal and opposite reaction (Newton's third law). For every pain there is a pleasure in the synchronous moment. There is a synchronous drawback for every benefit, an equal and opposite negative for every positive, equal and opposite losses and gains. For every moment you perceive challenge, there is an equal and opposite support and a blessing for every stressor. Every equal and opposite reaction takes place in synthesis and synchronicity.

- Whatever we perceive in others we have in ourselves in similar or different forms. Everything you see is you! Life is your hall of mirrors, reflecting back to you the different perceptions, truths, and untruths you have of yourself.

"We can only change our lives and create a world of our own if we first understand how such a world is constructed, how it works, and the rules of the game," says author and business trainer Michael E. Gerber.

Develop the art of asking yourself high-quality questions, like:

- What are the blessings of your stressors?
- Who is supporting you when someone else is challenging you?
- What are you gaining equal to what you perceive you're losing?
- Who is praising you when someone else is criticizing you?
- What is the benefit equal to the drawback of what is happening to you?
- What is the positive equal to the negative?

Answering these quality questions leads you out of uncertainty into certainty as your mind starts to see the equal and opposite sides of what is happening or what has happened. In this way, you become the master of your destiny and not the victim of your history. By doing this, you take off your blindfold and see the beauty of your life.

CHAPTER 4

The Wealth Creator Extraordinaire as a Business Leader

A business genius understands that it is of high importance to be equally altruistic and narcissistic in your business. You run your business equally for yourself and for others. It is the way you serve the world. Nobody works or runs a business just for others. You do it equally for yourself. You also don't grow a business just for yourself. You grow it as a service to people. If your business does not offer a service to people, nobody will support your business because fair exchange cannot take place and you cannot have a lasting business nor create wealth.

Unlocking the Leader Inside

The secret to unlocking your business leadership is to know what your inspiration, intrinsic motivation, and burning desire of highest

43

importance is for how you want to serve the world through your business. The danger is that it's too easy to inject and project expectations you perceive others have of you. If you're unclear and uncertain about your own burning desires, you can easily take on the desires of others. It's easy for the first generation to have ideas, wishes, and dreams that the next generations will simply continue with the business and wealth the first generation created. It's difficult—sometimes bordering on impossible—for first-generation parents to have no vocational or business expectations of their children. When you're the founder and builder of a business or a collection of businesses and you've put your life's blood into growing and expanding the businesses for the purpose of creating family wealth, your wish and desire is for the next generations to continue with what you have created.

The challenge for the generations that follow is to be authentic to their dreams, wishes, and heart's desires. Another challenge is to find the roadmap and pathway to please both your first generation parents and yourself. If you live your life to fulfill your parents' wishes, you'll soon discover that you're harboring resentment, anger, bitterness, and discontentment. If you live your life to fulfill only your own wishes, with no regard for anyone else, you'll have to deal with guilt, fear, shame, and conflict. What then is the roadmap and pathway to your own unique business expression and creation? The pathway to your answer will be found in the following steps:

1. Be very honest with yourself when you ask yourself the following question: "*What is my burning desire and most specific wish for myself vocationally?*" Do what you love and love what you do. Every person has a calling, and listening to your calling is wisdom. Nobody can tell you what your service to the world should be. Only you can know it. Be authentic to yourself and do whatever it takes to put your unique and extraordinary stamp of service on the world.

2. How specifically will your burning desire and specific wish serve and benefit you? In other words, what will be the narcissistic benefits? Make a comprehensive list of all the benefits you'll gain when

you bring your form of service to the world. List the benefits for you in all areas of your life—namely spiritually, mentally, vocationally, financially, family-wise, socially, and physically. We bring meaning and purpose to our existence through the way we serve. That is the unique contribution we bring in being a living part of the world.

3. How specifically will your burning desire and specific wish serve and benefit others? In other words, what will be the altruistic benefits? Make a comprehensive list of all the benefits for others when you bring your form of service to the world. List the benefits for others in all areas of their lives, namely spiritually, mentally, vocationally, financially, family-wise, socially, and physically. See with certainty how your acts of service will enhance the lives of others.

4. Link the vocational expectations and wishes of your parents from the first generation to your burning desire and specific wish vocationally. Ask yourself the following questions and answer them enough times—until you can say with conviction and inspiration, "*I can see it!*" How specifically will I serve my first-generation parents when I follow my own career path? What will be the biggest benefits for them? How specifically will I serve my parents' highest values and priorities when I follow my own career path? How will my career path benefit my parents, my family, and me?

5. What is the most authentic legacy you wish to leave? Your legacy wish is an expression of the meaning, fulfillment, inspiration, and impact you wish to have for yourself as well as for others. Think out of the box and think without holding back. You are firstly accessing the big *why* of your acts of service. The *how* will appear as you start to take dedicated action steps.

6. What is the legacy the first generation wishes to leave? Link your legacy to the first generation's legacy and ask yourself: How specifically is my legacy helping my previous generation's legacy, and how specifically is their legacy helping my legacy? You're not serving as an island. You're serving as a part of the whole. Each individual contribution is equally important.

7. What do you believe your life purpose and mission is vocationally? What, in other words, do you wish to dedicate your career to? Do you wish to do it because you believe that's your purpose and mission? No matter how big or small you perceive your vocational life purpose and mission is, it's important. Give yourself permission to serve others according to your purpose. A multinational successful businessperson and full-time parent in a family play equally important roles. Both these roles are equally needed as acts of service in the world.

8. How will your life purpose and mission serve your first generation, the world, and yourself? Own your power and contribution and be authentic. Your acts of service in your own way and according to your hierarchy of values are needed. No act of service is mediocre in comparison to another act of service.

Focus on serving in your unique way. The art of linking will take you on a different path of certainty than doing guesswork, which takes you on a path of uncertainty and doubt.

The pathway to a fulfilled, inspired, meaningful, and prosperous career is to be yourself, live your dream, and create your destiny. Linking your pathway to the pathway of your previous generation makes the most sense and will give you the certainty and freedom to live with authenticity and individuality as a valuable family member, serving your family and yourself. As I often tell my clients, follow Warren Buffett and tap dance to work everyday because you love what you do and you do what you love. You have and give meaning.

How to Be a Great Businessperson

Your greatness is part of you. Your greatness is locked into your vision, mission, and purpose, as well as in the way you express yourself according to your highest values, priorities, and what is of importance to you. Every businessperson you admire and look up to is a reflection of you. What you see in others you have in yourself. Your greatness is in your acts of service, no matter in what form or fashion. It's also in your self-belief, your self-concept, and your self-confidence that you're important and needed.

Your greatness is in the service you bring to your clients, customers, loved ones, and the world. A great businessperson focuses on service and then on how the service through fair exchange brings financial compensation. Also note that you equally serve by being an employer or an employee. Greatness is not in what you're doing. It's in how you're doing it. My dad raised my siblings and me with the following input: "It doesn't matter whether you're a street sweeper or own a business or a collection of businesses; it matters *how* you sweep the street or run the business. It's in your doing that your greatness or mediocrity shines through. No matter what you do, do it to the best of your ability."

Make a list of all the character traits and behaviors of the businesspeople you admire. Then own your form and expression of all these traits and behaviors. Cultivate a mindset and behavioral patterns that reflect your business ethos and the culture you wish to express. Know what you want and put in all the action steps that will help you to get there.

Decide to be the best you can be in the acts of service you wish to bring into your authentic form and expression. Plan the business you wish to build or the family business you wish to build further with care and wisdom. Ask for help, get a mentor to work with you, and work with a business plan and strategy. For the family business owner (oftentimes a first-generation family member), remember to work with a business plan and strategy to pass the torch you have ignited. You're not going to live forever and be a wise businessperson who knows when and how to let got and hand over. You've formed the snowball for your family. Learn wise ways to pass the snowball to the next generation so they can grow the snowball bigger that you have started.

Family Business Versus Own Business Versus Employee

There are so many wise choices for you to make in business. You might have one or many of the following choices:

- Work as an employee in a company not belonging to your family.
- Work as an employee in a company that belongs to your family.
- Take the torch from the igniter of the family business torch and be mentored and educated by the igniter of the family business.
- Build your own business, focusing on your service you wish to bring to the world.
- Buy a business from your family's collection of businesses.
- Take responsibility for the family's philanthropic cause.
- Take responsibility for your own philanthropic cause.
- Build the family as a form of business by being a full-time parent.

It is 100 percent your choice how you wish to bring your unique service to the world, irrespective of being a full-time artist, a businessperson, a philanthropist, or a full-time parent. Nobody can tell you what to do and if you follow the guidance of a parent or a friend, it means you're not connected to your purpose and the vision and mission you have for your life. Maybe you've never thought of yourself as a businessperson, but you see yourself as a budding actress or actor or a man or woman who takes care of the well-being of horses in your community.

The biggest waste of a beautiful life is sitting around and doing nothing. This leads to depression, alcoholism, or drug abuse because the person feeling empty will do anything to fill the emptiness and despair. Man's search for meaning is getting traction when you start to feel you make a difference to your own life as well as the lives of others. Everybody wishes to be loved, needed, and appreciated for who they are. You can be assured that taking the easy route and living off a family trust is going to be your downfall if you do not make meaning of your existence and fulfill your purpose for being alive. *Everybody is born with a purpose, and it is in your hands to decide what it is and live your meaningful life.*

If you're born into a family where you have choices of how you wish to serve the world, you're a fortunate person. Remember, you have not created your fortunate life, you were born into it and you have won the ovarian lottery. You're privileged. You have to prove to yourself that you're a worthy custodian to take the torch passed to you. The family wealth and family business passed to you belong to the family, and you're the custodian for the well-being of your family and yourself. Be a worthy custodian and get all the help you need to grow what's in your custody. Grow it with your uniqueness and your vision for it in combination with respectful consideration of the vision of your prior generation. Every generation comes with its own worldview, ideas, vision, mission, outlook on life, dreams, and goals. A family with powerful, inspired, meaningful, purposeful visions can pass those ideals on from generation to generation. *Remember that it's up to you, and only you, to live the life you want to live.*

A Reminder for First-Generation Business Owners

I address every business owner in the family, who will pass the torch to the next generation, when I say, "Congratulations on what you've achieved in your lifetime. You've worked hard, dreamt big, believed in yourself, and relentlessly pursued your roadmap to success for the sake of your family and yourself."

The hardest thing is to let go and allow others, maybe even some who are better and smarter than you, to take over what you've been building over many years. You might even be concerned that you're passing the torch to family members you believe are less intelligent and ill equipped to take over, but because they're family and you feel responsible, you know the torch will be passed to them.

I believe it's the desire of every parent to create an extraordinary life for their children. We want to give them more than what we perceived we had, and we want to make life easy and happy for our offspring. Ask parents what their wish is for their children, and the most common answer is "I want them to be happy." Parents want for their children what nobody has achieved yet, and that is a blissful life of pure happiness—living happily ever after. I believe our responsibility to our children is encapsulated in the following poem from *The Prophet* by Kahlil Gibran:

On Children

Your children are not your children.
They are the sons and daughters of life's longing for itself.
They come through you but not from you,
And though they are with you, yet they belong not to you.
You may give them your love but not your thoughts,
For they have their own thoughts.
You may house their bodies but not their souls,
For their souls dwell in the house of tomorrow,
which you cannot visit, not even in your dreams.
You may strive to be like them,
but seek not to make them like you.
For life goes not backward nor tarries with yesterday.
You are the bows from which your children
as living arrows are sent forth.
The archer sees the mark upon the path of the infinite,
and He bends you with His might
that His arrows may go swift and far.
Let your bending in the archer's hand be for gladness;
For even as He loves the arrow that flies,
so He loves also the bow that is stable.

It is the responsibility of every generation of parents to accept and appreciate the following:

- Every child born in your family is an individual and not an extension of any parent.
- Parents must be acutely aware of the danger and trap of living vicariously through their children.
- No child is born to live the dreams and goals of a parent. Every person is born to live his or her own dreams.

- Every person is born with his or her own unique purpose and mission. No person is born to fulfill the purpose and mission of another person, even if the other person is a beloved parent.
- The gift of love parents can give to their children is copious amounts of freedom to express and be themselves authentically, without conditions.
- As a parent, you must offer unconditional love and acceptance of every child, even when the child is the opposite of you.
- Dream and express your own dreams for yourself and leave your children to dream and express their own dreams.
- Educate your children with your wisdom and knowledge. Caringly be their mentor and not their judge. Be a "go-to-person" for them to receive wisdom and mentoring from. Offer advice and guidance only when they ask you for it.
- Cultivate a caring relationship with each of your children and let them take the lead in their lives; you follow.

The love and expectations a parent can have of their children can sometimes get mixed up. Your love for your child is not equal to what you expect of them. Your love is supposed to be unconditional. What you've built up for your family in all areas of life is your act of love to them. What they do with your gift of love is not a reflection of their love for you. Your son who chooses to follow a vocation you perceive to be wrong for him as a man is not a reflection of his love for you. Instead, it is a reflection of his dreams and expression of his life journey. *You have your own journey to follow in your life. You are not here to follow someone else's journey.*

CHAPTER 5

The Wealth Creator Extraordinaire as a Money Manager

The wealth creator and philanthropist Warren Buffett points out that one is lucky to be a winner of the "ovarian lottery." "I was born in 1930. I won the ovarian lottery," he says, using the catchy term he coined a few years ago. "I was born in the United States. I was born white. I was born male. I had all kinds of luck."

Being born into a family of wealth, with extraordinary opportunities for your education, health, and physical well-being, social connections, access to money, and access to the best of the best for personal development, makes you a winner of the ovarian lottery. You are one of the few fortunate ones on Earth who has been born with the proverbial "golden spoon in your mouth" and all you did was to be born. Gratitude for what you have will take you a long way; sadly, ingratitude and entitlement will make you an emotional sloth.

You're not responsible for the wealth your family possesses; your parents are, if they're the first-generation wealth creators. Maybe you're the third or fourth generation in your family, in which case you're even further removed from the family wealth creators. Their gift to you as the next generation is the wealth they created for your family. Your responsibility and gift back to the family is to be a worthy custodian of the family wealth, as well as a financial leader in growing the snowball of family wealth for your family for multiple generations.

Financial leaders show the following traits:

1. They place high value, importance, and priority on creating and growing wealth. When they do their value determination (as described in Chapter 2), they see with ease and certainty that wealth creation and growth are among their top five values and priorities and hold intrinsic importance to them.

2. They dedicate their lives to growing the perpetual motion of the family snowball of wealth. They understand that family wealth creation started as an idea and a desire coming from a perception and feeling of pain that wealth was absent in the family. They understand that wealth will grow only when there is a desire and action steps firmly in place to grow the snowball of wealth for the benefit of the family for generations to come.

3. They have a purpose and reason for creating and growing wealth for the family purse far beyond the accumulation of luxuries and material possessions. They have an affluent lifestyle, but they have a greater purpose for wealth creation. They have a purpose to serve mankind and give money where money is most needed and appreciated. They have a vision for the outreach, influence, and impact that wealth can have on society. Since only 1 to 3 percent of the world population has wealth freely available because they have an authentic value and the most aligned action steps for creating wealth, the gift of wealth creation and insight into having an aligned value system and behavior can generously be shared with those who never developed these important skills.

The most impactful way to share these skills is by investing in the education, health, and well-being of people. This costs a lot of money, but without the financial support for high-level education and access to good health care, the nation and the world will be a poor place. The purpose of wealth can range from providing jobs to improving education and health care availability. These leaders find a purpose bigger than material possession to significantly increase the fulfillment, meaning, inspiration, and prosperity of life.

4. They have wisdom of wealth, and they study the work of other wealth creators from before and now. They understand that wealth *wisdom* stands for the following:

   - Unlock your *w*ealth in all areas of life (spiritually, mentally, vocationally, financially, family, social, physical).
   - Live your *i*nspired life. Have clarity of your life vision and mission.
   - Deliver *s*ervice that you love. Do what you love and love what you do.
   - Know your burning *d*esires. Have certainty about your dreams and goals.
   - *O*utline your action steps. The physical universe applauds action, not thought.
   - Focus on *m*astery. Focus on life-long learning toward your own empowerment and self-mastery.

5. They have specific and well-defined goals and actions steps to execute their goals. They know with certainty what they wish to dedicate their lives to, and they do it without hesitation or making excuses. Life becomes a testimony to their dedication. They are known for their pursuit of financial wealth creation for their families and their own well-being and health. They have their priorities in place, and they plan their lives in the pursuit of their wishes and heart's desires. People turn to them for guidance, wisdom, information, and education. Their words and actions show clearly what they wish to achieve, and their achievements are congruent and

focused. They do not use imperatives like *should, would,* or *ought to* in their language about wealth creation. They're certain in their language and they have a love affair with wealth creation for the purpose of making a difference for their families, for others, and for themselves.

6. They have a burning desire to leave a legacy and to make a lasting impact through their dedication to create and grow wealth. They have certainty of the legacy they wish to leave, and they show it in their actions, language, and behavior. They develop a deep desire to understand human behavior to assist them in mastering their lives so they can be an example and role model for their family members for multiple generations. They have a legacy in mind for their families for multiple generations, and they develop an inspiring roadmap for passing the torch for generations to come. Their family knows the words and expression of the family legacy and feels inspired and privileged to be part of it. Their family wishes to be part of that legacy and see how it serves them.

7. They have a deep sense of gratitude for what they have and they live with grace and thankfulness. They see how challenges are part of the school of life that will bring the best out in them, and they don't moan or complain about the pains of life. They embrace pain and pleasure, losses and gains, and challenges and support in the pursuit of their self-mastery and they're grateful for it. They start and end their days with a sense of gratitude for what is and they inspire others with their attitude of gratitude. People flock to them because they're inspiring, uplifting, and balanced in their perceptions. They count their blessings and know it's by grace and hard work that they have what they have.

8. They have financial knowledge and focus. They study the great works of history and art from the past and the present, available to everyone who chooses to access them. They study wealth creators and their strategies and they develop their own strategies that will stand the test of time. They are updated about world affairs and they read and study avidly. Their studies are supported by

books about business, finance, and human behavior, and they love learning and expanding their knowledge. They study human behavior as it's exhibited in both business and finance, and they invest in themselves to gain ever more knowledge to empower themselves. They value self-mastery and the mastery of business and finance, and they perceive that the school of life is always in session. They do not feel saturated and have an ever-deepening hunger to know more, learn more, and read more. They perceive they are their own biggest asset and they relentlessly pursue knowledge, wisdom, and insight to empower themselves. They develop a certainty about their financial strategies and are not swayed by market philia or phobia. They have a razor-sharp focus on finance and business, and they will direct most conversations to speak about it. Their lives are a showcase of their focus, dedication, and perseverance.

What is your heart's desire for the wealth you either inherited or created yourself? Is it to have more material possessions, or is it far more than this? Is it to make a difference in the lives of others? Your choice will greatly influence the meaning and fulfillment you experience in your life. Therefore, choose wisely.

CHAPTER 6

The Wealth Creator Extraordinaire as a Family Leader

A family is *the* place where you have the right of belonging—simply through your birthright. There are two forms of family relationships: the first is family blood bonds—this is a relationship that comes from sharing the same parent or parents and coming from the same genetic pool. Your *blood bond* relationships are the ones you have with your grandparents, parents, brother(s), sister(s), and cousins. The second form of family relationship is created through a *bond of affinity*—belonging to the family through marriage or adoption into the family. The most important assets a family has are the family members, the human capital. Nothing is more important than the people—the men, women, and children that form a family. "The wealth of a family," says James Hughes, "consists of the human capital and intellectual capital of its members."

The most important human capital investment a person can make is to invest in her or himself. Your greatest asset is yourself. The second greatest human capital investment a person can make is in family relationships, both the members you have blood bonds with and the members with whom you share bonds of affinity. Untold pain is caused by strife, jealousy, resentment, bitterness, conflict, and rejection in family relationships. Countless songs of joy have been composed describing the blessings of kind and caring family relationships.

How to Build Powerful and Strong Family Relationships

Through my years of serving families as a family-focused psychologist and a family behavioral strategist, I've come to the following conclusions about ways to relate to family members:

- **Understand how to make relationships work and apply human behavioral skills.** Family leaders know each family member is a mirror for other members. They understand human behavior and they know every person has every character trait listed in the dictionary, and all family members will express their character traits in their own unique and individual way. They look with courage and wisdom in the mirror their family members hold up for them and they own their part and unique expression of the character trait they see in their family member, in themselves.
- **Remember that judgment and criticism are unwise.** Whatever you judge others for is a reflection of yourself. The more you try to run away from your shadow parts by pointing your finger at others, the more you stay in denial of the magnificence of human beings, yourself included. Rather, attempt on a daily basis to take responsibility for your actions, reactions, and behaviors. Develop the taste for mastering relationships and build strong and lasting relationships with all family members. If cash is king, then family is the emperor.

- **Keep on studying how to build strong family relationships for lasting generations**. Families are special and belonging to a family where there are good relationships is extra special. Having the vision to build strong family relationships for lasting generations is inspiring. Every couple who gets married and decides to have children have dreams of having a great family with a happily-ever-after marriage and kids who get on well. But the reality is that relationships are tricky and building good solid relationships take skills, know-how, and perseverance.

Carl Jung, the Swiss psychiatrist and psychotherapist who founded analytical psychology, said:

> One does not become enlightened by imagining figures of light but by making the darkness conscious. Until you make the unconscious conscious, it will direct your life and you will call it fate. Knowing your own darkness is the best method for dealing with the darkness of other people. Condemnation does not liberate, it oppresses. Everything that irritates us about others can lead us to an understanding of ourselves. The meeting of two personalities is like the contact of two chemical substances: if there is any reaction, both are transformed.
> **—Jung, C.G., 1933, *Modern Man in Search of a Soul*, Kegan Paul, Trench, Trüber and Co, London.**

Build Warm, Caring Relationships

There are three types of relationships: careful, careless, and caring. A *careful* relationship is when you walk on eggshells around the other one in the relationship. A wife too scared to speak her mind to her husband or a father too insecure to say no to his child because he does not want to lose favor with his child is building a careful relationship. *Too careful to be real* means you will battle to build a relationship of mutual respect and comfort and the relationship will be characterized by dishonesty and insecurity.

A *careless* relationship is a relationship characterized by treatment of the other person with actions and feelings showing you don't care about your effect on them. It's a husband not caring about the effect the long hours he spends watching or playing a sport have on the family; it's the child who does not care about the effect his rudeness has on his sibling. This is a relationship where the members of the family would prefer to be further apart from each other than close to each other.

A *warm and caring* relationship is characterized by caring about your impact on the other person. It's a relationship where you consider how your decisions, behavior, and actions affect the rest of your family. It's a father who understands when he plays golf on a Saturday that he gives his wife *time off* on Sunday while he takes the kids to the park so she can do something she likes. A caring relationship is built on the understanding of compromise and equal give and take.

It's human nature to fluctuate between careless and careful behavior because you become careless when you put yourself on the pedestal and the other person in the pit and you become careful when you put yourself in the pit and the other one on the pedestal. A warm and caring relationship is one in which you consider your family member as equal to you, even when the other one is your one-year-old child. All humans deserve to be treated with respect, dignity, and unconditional acceptance, which includes everyone in the family from newborn to adult.

Building strong and caring relationships takes time, effort, energy, wisdom, and love. It does not happen by itself; it follows a burning desire to have a great, strong, and caring family with strong relationships. Hold this as the vision for your family and expect nothing else but this for your family.

A wealth creator extraordinaire as a family leader understands the universal law that the natural state for everything is to be in balance, but people throw events, experiences, emotions, and circumstances in chaos (the opposite of balance and order) through their lopsided perceptions, unrealistic expectations, and ignorance about human behavior. A universal truth is that the sum of all family relationships are balanced and in homeostasis. This means that every family dynamic has a conservation of all human behavior traits and different family members express the whole spectrum of traits. For every family member who expresses the human trait of generosity, there is a family member who expresses the human trait of stinginess. For every family member who expresses the human trait of hard work and focus, there is a family member who expresses laziness and lack of focus. For every family member who expresses physical empowerment, fitness, and health with ideal weight, there is a family member who will be unfit, not healthy, and overweight.

At any moment in synthesis and in synchronicity, the group of family members will express all human behavior traits and the family members balance each other out. The collection of family members expressing all the human behavior traits is in reality expressing a portion of the universe. The collection of family members indeed is a micro universe all by itself. In the microuniverse you call your family, everything is present. Nothing is missing.

Value and Invest in Partnership as the Foundation of the Family

The day you get married to your spouse or the day you move in with your life partner, you do it with the wish and intention to be together until death parts you. Nobody gets married with the expectation that it won't last. It's hard work—it takes time, attention, and focus on the marriage to make it work. Since about half of marriages end in divorce, what can you do to make yours be part of the 50 percent that last forever? The first rule is to make your marital relationship or your life partnership the most important relationship as the foundation for the family relationships. How do you continue to build your relationship with the mate you've chosen for life? Love them for who they are, boots and all, and do not try to change them. You're in for endless frustration and resentment if you try to change your mate.

In 75 percent of marriages, the wife naturally and spontaneously takes care of the nurturance of the family, its physical well-being, and its social life. She looks after the house, the pets, the garden; she buys the groceries, arranges the kids' play dates, and remembers the birthdays of family and friends. In these 75 percent of marriages, the husband naturally and spontaneously takes care of the safety and security of the family by providing financially through his career. He pays for the family home, provides for its future financial well-being through his investment portfolio and business endeavors, pension fund, and retirement annuities, and he runs the family budget.

This doesn't mean wives don't contribute financially; it means these husbands make it possible for the wives to focus on the areas of the family life they naturally and spontaneously like to take care of. When the wife takes care of the well-being and nurturance of the family and kids, it gives the husband the freedom to focus on what he naturally and spontaneously likes to focus on. Be grateful for each other and express your thankfulness regularly.

Eight Keys to a Successful Marriage

When you're in a good period in your marriage, you usually think it's great to be married and you feel you're one of the lucky ones who will "live happily ever after." If you are in a bad spell in your marriage, you easily feel your life is a nightmare and you wish you could change your partner. Most people wish to be married and certainly wish for a happy and successful marriage. Here are the eight key guidelines I believe lead to a successful marriage.

Love Your Partner for Who He or She Is

Everybody wants to be loved for who they are and nobody wants to be criticized for who they are. We each have our own unique set of values or priorities or things that are important to us. Nobody has exactly your set of values or priorities and that is what makes you unique. There is nobody like you and nobody like your partner. You got attracted to your partner for the ways they are the same as you *and* for the ways they are the opposite of you.

Paul and Arlene, a couple married for eight years, learned how to love each other for who they are. Paul loves sports, both watching sports on television and playing sports, and Arlene loves reading and studying self-help books. Once they linked their high values and priorities to each other, they understood that by being true to themselves, they give the other one the freedom to be true to themselves. While Paul is watching or playing sports, Arlene has the freedom to read her books and study her self-help courses. Both Paul and Arlene put the effort in to love each other for who they are, because they both value their relationship.

Plant Flowers in Your Mind about Your Partner

Your mind is a powerful tool you can use, but an ungoverned mind becomes a weapon of destruction. When you think negative things about your partner and fill your mind with everything they do wrong, you plant weeds in your mind. And weeds have the habit of growing fast and taking over. Thoughts of anger, aggression, blame, criticism, and negativity poison your mind about the person.

Every person has a balance of positive and negative traits. When you focus more on negative traits, the positive traits are obscured. Make it a healthy habit to remind yourself of what you like and love about your partner. Plant flowers in your mind about your partner. This is a lifelong investment in your marriage. When you're grateful for something, you receive more of it. Speak words of life into your relationship.

Understand What Drives Your Partner

Opposites attract, and what drives your partner will most likely be something that does not really drive you. Maybe your partner is driven by her motherly instincts to look after the children and create a beautiful home while you're driven by your business. We make each other possible in a relationship. A contented marital partner will keep asking, "How does my life partner make me possible?" The two opposites make a whole, and with your partner you create your whole marriage by your differences and similarities. Accept what drives your partner by considering how the things that drive them benefit you.

Be Best Friends and Have Each Other's Back

There is nobody you like as much as your partner; otherwise, you wouldn't have chosen to marry and create a life together. Remember that. Of all the millions of people on this planet, you chose each other because you perceived far more likes than dislikes in each other. There is nobody you spend more time with. Give your partner what he or she wants and your partner will give you what you want. That's the law of fair exchange. Look out for each other, play together, and laugh together. You'll have to go far to find another friend so dedicated to you.

Develop a Healthy Intimate Life

Intimacy is the cement of a relationship—as long as it's seen only as one important part, rather than the only important part. Many people develop fantasies or nightmares about their sex lives. Intimacy in a relationship works like a seesaw; one partner wants it more than the other one, and then it shifts and the other one wants it more. There is no magic formula of frequency; the only answer is what works for both of you. Open and honest communication of what you like and dislike and aiming to bring pleasure to your partner will bear fruit. Sex is a driving force, and when there is a perception of a void, it can cause stress and tension. Develop a healthy sex life that brings both joy and closeness.

Create Surprises and Fight Complacency

If you know what your partner likes, surprise them unexpectedly with a love gift, even if it's only a favorite chocolate. Create traditions in your relationship that communicate the message that you appreciate and value each other. Learn to speak the love language of your partner and help your partner to know what your love language is. It does not matter what it is; it's unique to you and your life partner's love language is unique to them. If you do for your partner what's important to them, your partner will do the same for you. Everybody likes to be appreciated.

Have Realistic Expectations

Know your partner, love your partner, and appreciate your partner. Your partner is not you; your partner has unique thoughts, ideas, likes, and dislikes. If you wish to change the person into who you want your partner to be, you're creating unrealistic expectations, and you'll soon feel angry, bitter, and challenged. Keep on asking the quality question: "How does the person my partner is benefit and serve me in what's important to me?" Stop injecting and projecting your values and priorities onto your partner; accept your partner as your complementary opposite.

Life is not a fairytale, but you can create your happily ever after with the right mindset, action steps, and desire to have the marriage that brings out the best in both of you. To be loved and to love is one of life's greatest gifts to mankind.

Do Life Together

Do things together and separately, give each other special and focused time and keep some time for yourself and your interest and priorities. In other words, have *we* time, *family* time, and *me* time. The moment your cup seems empty because you're giving too much of yourself to others in your family, you tend to become angry, bitter, and resentful, and you can even become depressed. Count your blessings in your marriage or relationship and compare it to your own goals and wishes for your marriage or relationship. Guard against comparing it to other relationships. You'll never know what happens in those so-called perfect marriages behind the closed doors of their family homes.

Traits of a Family Leader

One of the most important action steps you can focus on in building strong family relationships is to accept each member of the family for their uniqueness and individuality. This section looks at traits of extraordinary family leaders.

Family Leaders Know Everyone Wants to Be Loved for Who They Are

Each person, young and old, wants to be loved for who they are and not for what they do. A mother asked me how she should handle her two-year-old son who was showing lots of anger. He shouted a lot and hit his four-month-old sister. The mother also told me he had started going to a playgroup three mornings a week, began sleeping in his big bed, and had begun potty training. Put yourself in the shoes of this two-year-old and see from his point of view how many changes he's dealing with.

Loving him for who he is does not mean accepting his anger and his shouting; loving him for who he is means understanding that no child of two years has the skills to deal with all these changes. Give him your heart, not your resentment. When you put him in your heart and give him the message that you care for him, you understand him, and you're there for him, you put down more building blocks in building a strong relationship with him. When you parent from your heart, you become more caring toward your child and the child feels loved, understood, and cared for.

I advised the mother of this two-year-old to spend special one-on-one time with him and join him in doing what he likes doing. Let him know you understand it's hard for him to have all these new things in his life, but you'll help him, you love him, and you're there for him. Focus on building a caring relationship with your family members instead of just focusing on correcting behavior.

Family Leaders Build Family Memories through Traditions, Celebrations, and Rituals

What do you want your children and spouse to remember about being part of the family? What are the special celebrations, traditions, and rituals you want to create for your family to build strong relationships and a strong sense of belonging? My family is creating beautiful memories through annual family holidays; outings on Sundays (our family day); rituals on birthdays, Mother's Day, Father's Day; end-of-year acknowledgments and ceremonies of growth and improvement (we acknowledge each member in our family for their growth and areas of improvement and accomplishment during a family award ceremony at the end of each year); and family nights of making beds on the floor and watching movies together. Create your own unique family memories by having your own unique family celebrations, traditions, and rituals. They glue family relationships strongly.

Take lots of family photos and surround your family with reminders of good times together. Good times can be captured in photos. Tell your kids as they grow older the stories of your life together and convey the message of *us*. Build the family team with a team spirit. I will never forget how my mother regularly reminded us that our family should "keep your heads up high and face life with courage." I've reminded myself of this through the many years since childhood. This is the family motto we all carry in our hearts.

A Wealth Creator Extraordinaire as a Family Leader Understands the Uniqueness of Everyone

Such wealth creators understand that every family member will be their own unique expression of what they value most as their most important and highest priority—that to which they choose to dedicate their time, energy, attention, focus, and intention.

Whether it's business, finances, physical health, fitness and vitality, the family relationships and caretaking, social networking, or spirituality—whatever each individual family member chooses as their expression of value and importance—the family leader accepts it without expectations. They learn the art of communicating in the family member's language and they guard themselves from the risk of unrealistic expectations. They understand that human behavior is consistent and universal and that every man, woman, and child will lead their lives in the pursuit of what they value as most important and of highest priority. Expecting others to be who you are will be met with resistance. When you accept a person for who they are, you will be met with open arms.

A Wealth Creator Extraordinaire as a Family Leader Understands that Every Family Member Has a Unique Life Purpose, Mission, and Vision

Every family member, regardless of whether they belong to the family through blood bonds or bonds of affinity, lives to pursue the fulfillment of the wishes and dreams they have for their lives. Whether they're conscious or not of their life purpose and mission, every man, woman, and child is living life in the pursuit of fulfilling the purpose that achieves their mission. A family that gives members the permission, support, and encouragement to be authentic to what is of highest value, importance, and priority to them, is a powerful family with deep understanding of human behavior.

The first generation gave itself permission to be authentic to what they wished for. The same allowance is important for every generation that follows. The most powerful families, lasting for multiple generations, are the families who have the mindset that allows freedom of self-expression within the containment of the family as a whole. The family as a whole becomes a cosmos of the expression of life purposes, missions, and visions that creates a family universe of unique, empowered, inspired, fulfilled, meaningful, and prosperous individuals. A family with this culture has the greatest potential to last for multiple generations. "The mission of family governance," says James Hughes, "must be the enhancement of the pursuit of happiness of each individual member."

A Wealth Creator Extraordinaire as a Family Leader Understands the Essence and Importance of Family Time Together

They have a keen understanding that the most dynamic way to build strong relationships also depends on spending time together. Since a family can be seen as both a business and a social enterprise, spending time together can take on different forms:

- **Social time—having fun and playtime together.** Someone in the family will have it as a high priority and interest to create and arrange playtime together. Acknowledge this person and give him or her the *position* of family social director. Light-hearted fun and special moments together bind a family together through many generations.
- **Business time—meeting to discuss the different family-as-a-business issues.** Family governance can be determined, honored, and kept alive and well structured through these times together. The purpose of family governance is to have a successful, decision-making system as well as a foundation for the culture, mindset, human behavior skills, and vision for the family in perpetuity.
- **Growth time.** Time needs to be spent together focusing on education in the many different aspects of the family affairs, affecting all generations. It's essential to educate the next generation about family affairs, the content and context of the family wealth, the dreams and goals, and their legacy and impact. If all of these are kept secret from family members, with only a privileged handful of family members having insight into them, the responsibility is heavily shifted onto the shoulders of a few while many lives remain in ignorance. Every family member has the right to information, knowledge, and insight about family affairs. Without openly sharing and educating the next generation, having a powerful generational family will remain wishful thinking.
- **Family retreats and meetings.** Can you imagine your family in this setting? It's a beautiful summer day and cars are busy arriving at the family estate. As every car comes to a stop, adults and children spill out. Excitement is in the air. Big hugs and smiles electrify the day. This is your family, all arriving for the annual family retreat—the highlight of the family calendar and not to be missed by anyone. Everyone knew the date of the annual family retreat weekend a year

in advance, and it was marked on everyone's calendar as high priority. The atmosphere is one of love, acceptance, and anticipation.

The annual family retreats are an important ingredient in the well-being of the family as a whole. This is the time when the family governance is revisited, the family stories are told and remembered, the family vision and mission is remembered and linked to everyone's personal vision and mission, the family balance sheet is updated, and philanthropic outreach is expanded. The meeting is inspiring and meaningful because everyone is reminded of the significant role they play in building this powerful family and how the sum is possible only because of the many parts. The human capital, mental capital, and financial capital of the family are revisited, the family balance sheet is revisited and updated, and plans and action steps for the following year are decided. Children and adults attend the retreat and after the family meeting, playtime begins.

Family retreats are some of the most important building blocks for your powerful family for generational impact. Relationships are strengthened and rekindled, inspiration is enhanced, and new insights and action plans are ignited.

How to Organize Family Retreats

If your family has not had any family meetings yet and you're inspired to be the founder of the annual family retreats, you'll want to consider the following suggestions from James Hughes, offered in his book *Family Wealth*.

Establish the family mission statement, because the family needs to understand its purpose. In preparation for establishing a family mission statement, Hughes suggests that every family member contribute to forming a common vision for the family, share certain values, acknowledge its *secrets*, recount the family history, choose a form of governance, and understand his or her role in the family.

Hughes suggests the following steps in preparing a family mission statement:

1. Agree to certain important rules for conducting family meetings.
2. For a family's first meeting on governance, each family member prepares a personal resume. The preparation of personal resumes gives each family member a chance to look at who he or she is and to share that view with the other family members. These resumes should include everything every family member believes a best friend might know about them and adds insight to the human capital of the family balance sheet.
3. Every family member prepares a personal mission statement, because it's easier to prepare a family mission statement when every adult family member is aware of his or her personal mission statement.
4. Each family member writes the ten top values considered most crucial to the family's long-term success. These values are to be displayed to everyone present. The values that reflect family consensus are compiled into the family mission statement.
5. Each family member should write what each would, at the age of 105 years, tell her or his immediate family was most important to him or her in life. This is to stimulate long-term thinking and help in creating the family mission statement.
6. Every family member writes a description of the family twenty years hence. This exercise makes family members begin to understand the long-term nature of the process they're undertaking.
7. A small committee (as decided by the family) writes a brief family history of the challenges and supports of the family as well as a description of the personalities of the famous or infamous ancestors whose impact is still felt.
8. The family creates its own governance as a description and outline of the self-governance of the family for posterity.

For subsequent family retreats and meetings, the following are important aspects to consider:

- Revisit the governance of the family and remind every family member why the family is functioning like a successful and productive business.
- The purpose of the family gets emphasized and every family member gets the opportunity to evaluate how each one has been supported and/or challenged by the family mission statement.
- Every family member shares a personal mission statement and a personal resume to update the family balance sheet regarding the human capital.
- The wealth of the family in all areas of human, social and financial capital, gets to be shared and the family financial statements to be circulated.
- Decisions get discussed and decided according to the joint-decision-making clause in the family governance.
- The shared family values are updated.
- The assessment of the personal growth to live meaningful, purposeful, and fulfilled lives is done for every family member.
- Family meetings and retreats are also about the narrative of the family—the stories of the past (where do we come from) to the stories of the present and future (where are we going).
- Family retreats and meetings must accommodate all the different generations as well as bonds of affinity.
- Family retreats and meetings without team building and laughter will soon create resistance for attendance from some if not most family members. The purpose of family meetings and retreats is to build a powerful family for posterity and invest in the ultimate well-being of every family member.

A family with the vision and mission for generational posterity invests in the human capital of the family—the men, women, and children in the family. Building long-lasting and caring relationships is a top priority, and the family members are willing to do whatever it takes to build a powerful family.

A Wealth Creator Extraordinaire as a Family Leader in a Second Marriage Knows How to Handle a Partner's Children

Put yourself in your partner's shoes and look at your actions and responses toward your partner's children. Does your partner look at you and feel loved and cared for in the way you treat these children, or does your partner look at you and feel resentment and disappointment in the way you treat the children? Remember, you are the adult, and you are *not* in competition with the children. An adult's love for another adult is completely different from an adult's love for a child. You cannot compare the two.

Work on becoming friends with the children. They already have parents and you cannot replace them. If you're too harsh in your criticism on how your partner is handling the children, you'll alienate your partner and he or she will pull away from you. If you discipline the children without having a relationship with them, they will resent you and reject you. Try to leave the discipline to the biological parent and refrain from being the wise parent who knows everything. Your partner does not want to hear about how undisciplined and unruly his or her kids are. Give the children time to build a relationship with you and be patient.

Curb your jealousy when your partner gives his or her children attention. Be realistic. Your partner's interest and love for you is separate from the interest and love expressed to the children. If you become a nag and insecure and moody when your partner's kids are with you, your partner will find you painful to be with, and that can be the beginning of the end of the relationship. Get your mind right: Your partner is a parent and your lover, and both play a role in your life. Ask yourself how it helps you to see your partner acting as a good father or mother.

Allow your partner time with his or her children. They might not see each other on a daily basis (depending on custody rights).

Give yourself permission to do something you like to do and give your partner some time alone with the children. In this way, you feel self-nurtured and your partner feels like a good parent. Be grateful for the times you have alone and go into your family mode when the children are with you. Both parts can be fulfilling.

Allow your partner to parent the children in their own way; give your advice caringly and realistically. Parents do the best they can with what knowledge they have. It's too easy to stand on the outside and give advice, but advice can easily be seen as criticism, and that is toxic for the relationship. Make sure your advice is given with care and love and not as a criticism.

Acknowledge that your partner feels guilty toward his or her children for many reasons. Divorced parents might feel guilty about being an absent parent. Guilt makes all people compensate; therefore, be patient with overcompensation. They're doing the best they can, and your support and understanding will go a long way. Children that are at the receiving end of overcompensation learn to manipulate masterfully and can become spoiled. It's not the child's fault, so try not to take it out on the child. Rather, try to be more understanding to your partner.

In the end, ask yourself the following question: Is this relationship important enough for me to put in the effort to integrate the children into my life—for a lifetime? If the answer is yes, then put in the effort. If the answer is no, then get out of the relationship. Do not make your partner choose between you and the children. You might come second.

A Wealth Creator Extraordinaire as a Family Leader Builds Strong Relationships with Children

Every family has a reason for being together. For instance, the Hindu religion believes that children choose their parents to enable them to learn the lessons they most need to learn to develop optimally. Aristotle claimed that man's highest calling is the pursuit of happiness, and in my years of working with families, I have yet to meet a parent who does not wish happiness for his or her children. What I wish for my children is more than happiness. I wish for my children to live lives of fulfillment, meaning, inspiration, purpose, and impact.

The wonder of love between generations is what makes a family wealthy. Wealth is a culmination of memories, special moments, kind words being shared, and love that transcends time, space, life, or death. The wonder of love can be felt in families for many generations, for it is love that builds your powerful family.

CHAPTER 7

The Wealth Creator Extraordinaire as a Social Leader

Every person is a leader in the areas of what he or she considers to be of highest importance, priority, and value. Don't let anyone make you believe you're not a leader. You *are* a leader and you choose the area of your life you wish to lead. The amazing thing in families is that in almost every generation someone rises up as a leader, leading the family either from in front or from behind. A leader is the one who takes the most responsibility for assuming the lead and inspiring followers to achieve goals and objectives that are most congruent to the whole. The leader also holds the big picture and sees the detail that needs to be in place for the big picture to realize.

A leader knows how to lead herself or himself. This is an important first step to authentic leadership: you take the lead in your own life before you start to lead others. The authentic way you take control of your own life is to first know what your burning desires are for your life and the burning desires you have for yourself.

Guideposts for Leading

The following are important questions to ask yourself. They will provide direction as you formulate a leadership game plan.

Question 1: What is My Vision and Mission?

Question 1. If I want to *lead as a visionary*, with a vision and a mission for a cause bigger than myself, what is my vision and mission, and what is the outreach of my vision and mission? Is the influence of my vision and mission local, national, global, galactic, or astronomical? Do I want to lead because I feel called to my vision and my mission? The more you can honestly and authentically answer these questions, the more you'll connect with your individual and personalized form of leadership. This form of leadership inspires and intrinsically motivates others to follow you because you make them feel good about themselves and offer meaning to others. Most people wish to make a difference, and when you lead by making others feel they make a difference, you become an inspired leader with inspired followers.

Question 2: What Am I Doing to Learn *Mastery of My Mind*?

What am I doing to take lead of my mind instead of allowing my mind to lead me? One important choice you have in life is how you use the power of your mind, because you can choose for your mind to overpower you or you can choose to learn techniques, actions, skills, and approaches to take control of your mind. You can also allow the challenges and pains of life to overwhelm you, or you can adopt a more masterful mindset by equilibrating your mind by changing your perceptions. The most dynamic way of changing your perceptions was discussed in Chapter 3, and this is a powerful way to take leadership of your thoughts, feelings, emotions, and perceptions.

How to Handle the Curve Balls

I've heard it said that "Sometimes the strongest person is the one who loves beyond all faults, cries behind closed doors, and fights battles that nobody knows about." Everybody knows what a curve ball is. It doesn't matter how well we prepare ourselves, how positive we try to be, how resilient we are in the face of the unexpected, when a challenge comes our way, it remains tough and can be painful. If we could change how life works, we would probably like to have a life of pleasure, support, ease, and fun. Just imagine how delightful that would be—no worries, no problems, no concerns.

But life is not designed like that. We all face times of fun and lightness and stress and heaviness. It's during difficulties, however, that we discover more about our ability to be strong, courageous, handle stress, and discover who is really there for us. Greek philosopher Aristotle said that humans grow maximally when they are on the cusp or border of challenge and support, chaos and order. But in moments of chaos and challenge we most likely will feel blinded to the support and order available for us.

Therefore, I wish to encourage you to adopt the following approach: When the rain storms at you, when it feels like someone has picked up a big hammer and decided to use it on you, when your heart feels heavy and you doubt your ability to cope, stop. Stop and ask yourself, Who is supporting me? Who is there for me? That person may be a phone call, a "please help me" away. You'll see you're *not* alone, you're not at the mercy of challenge, and you're receiving the grace of support just as much as you're receiving the pain of challenge.

Stop and count at least ten blessings to help you to shift your negative and heavy perceptions. Stop and find at least ten pleasures available to you. Maybe it's the warmth of your room, the sun shining outside, the great computer you're typing on, your full tummy after a meal, the taste of cool water in your mouth, the text message from a caring friend. Look until you can find enough to shift your heavy perceptions.

Find the blessings in the stressors; otherwise, you'll feel heavy and not light, sad and not glad, sorry for yourself and not grateful for every opportunity to learn to be more of what you would love to be and less of what you don't want to be. This battle against despair and heaviness is a big battle to face and to learn to conquer one step at a time. But it is a battle worth fighting. *Take leadership of your mind!*

Question 3: What Kind of Leadership Do I Want to Practice?

What kind of leadership do I wish to take in my choice of career or vocation? Do I want to lead from "in front" of do I want to lead "from behind"? These two forms of leadership are equally important. Your leadership from in front is more visible and pulls followers in the direction you wish to go. Leading from behind is less noticeable. You guide people to go where they wish to go.

Your form of leadership will be in the areas of your desire and the focus you wish to offer as an act of service to humanity. No matter what the act of service is, as long as it is what you love to do and fills you with intrinsic motivation and inspiration, your natural leadership in the area of your service will follow.

If you wish to consciously develop your natural leadership abilities in your vocation, consider these eight important guidelines:

- Guideline 1: Choose role models and study them.
- Guideline 2: Read ferociously about the topic and study leadership.
- Guideline 3: Own the traits of the greats.
- Guideline 4: Know yourself and be yourself.
- Guideline 5: Understand human behavior.
- Guideline 6: Have a heart for service.
- Guideline 7: Never give up.
- Guideline 8: Think out of the box and step out of your comfort zone.

Question 4: What Are My Social Leadership Dreams?

Ask yourself questions about what social cause, problem, or challenge you're interested in and would wish to tackle in finding solutions. It can be on any level you wish it to be, irrespective of the outreach. You can wish to make a difference in your friendship circle, your community, your town or city, your province or county, your country, your continent, the world, or even as far out as the galaxy. It's your choice.

Tips for Leaders

Every person has great self-worth and self-esteem; it might just be hidden a bit—or a lot. If you have moments of self-doubt and you are uncertain about your ability to make an impact and have social influence, apply the following tips to take your great self-worth and self-esteem out of their hiding place and show them with pride.

Tip 1: Understand Your Authentic Value System

Unpack your self-worth and self-esteem in your highest priorities and values. What makes people function is your values—that is, what's valued as having high priority and importance. You have your own unique set of values and priorities to live your life by. In your highest values, you're spontaneously inspired from within to take action. Your highest value is intrinsic; it's in you.

Anytime you do what you value highly and you're congruent with your values, you raise your self-worth. When you walk your talk, your belief strengthens and your self-worth increases. Your self-worth is stronger as your actions become more congruent with your values. Your natural born leadership is awakened when you're congruent with your values. Bottom line: your self-worth increases when your actions are congruent with your highest values.

Tip 2: Set Goals Congruent with Your Highest Priorities and Values

Self-esteem and self-confidence strengthen with an increase in self-worth, and your self-worth increases as you have clarity about your hierarchy of values and set realistic goals according to *your* hierarchy and not someone else's hierarchy of values. When you set goals congruent with your highest values, you have the highest probability of success. When you experience the *ABCDs* of negativity—feeling angry, bitter, challenged, and depressed—you're receiving feedback that confirms you're setting goals incongruent with your values.

Every time you envy someone and imitate them, you create a fantasy and you live with pseudo self-worth. Your self-esteem is reduced, you create suffering, and you become ungrateful. Set your goals according to *your* hierarchy of values, not someone else's.

Tip 3: Compare Yourself with Yourself

You grow your self-worth by being authentic to your hierarchy of values. This makes you a magnet; people feel safe around you and want to be closer to you. When you're authentic and true to your values, you become magnetic and influential and you attract opportunities. Compare yourself to your own goals, action steps, and the dreams you've set for yourself. Comparing yourself to someone else—who has a different hierarchy of values—is emotional suicide. "Envy is ignorance; imitation is suicide," said Ralph Waldo Emerson. How true these words are, and how futile it is to compare yourself to someone who has different values and priorities.

Tip 4: Focus on the *One Thing*

Ask yourself every day what steps are the highest priority for you to take to live your highest values. Ask just for that day. Determine the most common priority steps you're likely to take and determine your high-priority steps.

You have the most self-worth when you focus on high-value priorities because the rest of your life gets more ordered and organized and you attract more opportunities in your hierarchy of values. To achieve the results you desire, you must choose what matters most and give it all the time it demands. Ask yourself what is the *one thing* you can do that would mean the most to you and the impact and influence you want to have in your world.

Tip 5: Do Something Extraordinary on This Planet

You wake up your authenticity when you live your life according to your highest values, or telos, because your telos is the most meaningful, fulfilling, most loved thing for you to do. Your self-worth, self-esteem, and self-confidence is highest when you're driven by your purpose, whether it is to be a great mother/father for your kids, a successful entrepreneur, a supportive wife, a great friend, or the inventor of a new health product.

The truth about success and subsequent self-worth is directly linked to your ability to achieve extraordinary results in the future by stringing together powerful moments, one after the other. Putting together a life of extraordinary results simply comes down to getting the most out of what you do, when what you do matters to you. What do you consider extraordinary?

Shaping Your Legacy

Synonyms for *legacy* include words like gift, inheritance, share, heirloom, and aid. The legacy you wish to leave is the gift you wish to leave, or your inheritance and heirloom. It is your share of your talents and experiences that you wish to pass on as an aid to those following you in the next generations. It's no small task to leave a legacy, but it's as personal as your thumbprint, your heart's desire of what you want to be remembered for, and what influence you want to leave as your footprint.

As the starting member of your family, you might want to create a wealthy family in all seven areas, not only for one generation but for generations to come. You can make a real difference in somebody's life by leaving them a generous legacy. What is the family legacy you would love to leave for future generations? What is your burning desire for future generations? Do you want to be the inspiration for a wealthy family, empowered in all areas on the wheel of life? Do you want to create family wealth for generations to ensure opportunities and financial support in generational family members' pursuit of happiness and prosperity?

Formulating a family legacy does not happen overnight; nor does it happen without deep thinking and a big-picture vision. If it were in your hands and you could create a mission statement for your generational family for the next 100 years or even the next thousand years, what would your mission statement look like for future generations? That is the starting point of creating your family legacy.

Your legacy and gift to the world is directly proportionate to your hierarchy of values and your vision and purpose. If you have a high value and priority for a spiritual vision and mission, your legacy will be a spiritual legacy. An example of a spiritual legacy is Mother Theresa. She founded the Missionaries of Charity, a Roman Catholic religious congregation. It runs homes for people dying of HIV/AIDS, leprosy, and tuberculosis; soup kitchens; dispensaries and mobile clinics; children's and family counseling programs; orphanages; and schools.

If you value your mental empowerment and your focus and attention is on your mental mastery, then you'll leave a mental legacy. A mental legacy will be inclusive of anything educational, a mental model, or a mental solution. The psychologist Carl Jung left the legacy of analytical psychology and the use of archetypes. Thousands of psychologists and psychotherapists worldwide use his mental model in the professional assistance they offer to the world.

If you a have a high value, priority, and importance on building a business and providing employment to many people, you'll leave a business legacy to the world, either in the form of a business, a collection of businesses, or a brilliant mindset on how to be in the driver's seat of a successful business.

The Rockefeller family is an American industrial, political, and banking family that made one of the world's largest fortunes in the oil business during the late nineteenth and early twentieth centuries, with John D. Rockefeller and his brother William Rockefeller, primarily through Standard Oil. The family is also known for its long association with and control of Chase Manhattan Bank. They are considered to be one of the most powerful families, if not the most powerful family, in the history of the United States. Businesspeople worldwide still study John D. Rockefeller for his brilliant business mind and his ability to identify a significant void people have. He brought oil to America and had a significant impact on the change in lifestyle for millions of families.

With a high value and vision to build vast fortunes, you'll dedicate your life to building wealth for your family, your community, your country, and even for the world.

An example of a man who left a financial legacy is Mayer Amschel Rothschild, born in 1744. He passed his business legacy onto his five sons, Amschel, Salomon, Nathan, Carl, and James, who together built a significant global business in the financial services. Their business legacy has stretched over multiple generations, and the Rothschild business encompasses a diverse range of fields, including financial services, real estate, mining, energy, mixed farming, wine, and charities.

With a high value on family and dedicating your life to building a powerful family with significance and influence, you'll leave your legacy to your family. It means your actions, decisions, priorities, focus, and service will be to build a powerful family. Your words and actions will reflect your vision to build a powerful family. Any mother and/or father who leaves a legacy of empowering next generations is an example of leaving a family legacy. Rose Kennedy has been quoted as saying, "I dedicate my life to raising world leaders," and the Kennedy family was prominent in American politics, public service, and business during the twentieth century. At least one Kennedy family member held national elective office in every year between 1947 and 2011, a span of time comprising more than a quarter of the United States' existence.

If you have it in your heart and vision to leave a social legacy, your leadership ability will get stronger on a social level. Your life will show evidence that you're dedicating your time, energy, attention, and intention to a social cause.

The actress Audrey Hepburn starred in some of the most beloved films of the Golden Age of Hollywood—*Roman Holiday, Sabrina,* and *Breakfast at Tiffany's.* She also touched millions of lives through her philanthropic efforts. In her lifetime, Hepburn spent long periods of time visiting African nations and bringing food and water to children in war-torn places through UNICEF. She also visited Vietnam to bring awareness on immunization and initiate clean-water programs. Hepburn was appointed Goodwill Ambassador of UNICEF for her many years of service to the organization, spending time with the poor and underprivileged personally.

If you place a high priority and value on physical health and well-being and you dedicate many hours of your life on studying and researching health and well-being, your physical vision and mission most likely will influence your legacy. Think of the impact and influence you wish to have on the world and what legacy of health and well-being you wish to leave. What physical void do you wish to fill in your family, community, city, country, continent, or the world?

The modern-day Olympic Games were inspired by the ancient Olympic Games, which were held in Olympia, Greece, from the eighth century BC to the fourth century AD. Baron Pierre de Coubertin founded the International Olympic Committee (IOC) in 1894. The legacy of the Olympic Games is repeated every four years, and thousands of athletes compete and showcase their physical gifts and talents. The South African cardiac surgeon, Chris Barnard, performed the world's first successful human-to-human heart transplant in 1967. The legacy he left the world still saves lives worldwide daily.

What legacy do you wish to build and dedicate your life to and leave to your loved ones and to the world? You're not alive for no reason. Your influence and impact are needed, and only you can have this sphere of impact and influence, expressed through your uniqueness and authenticity. It starts small and grows as you grow. Nothing is too insignificant or too small. Everything starts as a thought, and by your actions you will transform the energy of your thoughts and wishes into matter and physical form. I strongly believe that your legacy is one of the important puzzle pieces in your powerful family's generational impact and influence.

Philanthropy, a Thinking Man's Gift to the World

If you're reading this book as the member of a family with wealth, you're probably one of the lucky ones who've won Warren Buffett's ovarian lottery. Are you born into a family with wealth and have access to more opportunities and experiences than most? Have you been born into a family on which the custody of great fortunes has been bestowed? If you're aware of the joy of receiving, you'll equally be aware that the joy of giving and giving back to others has a cascading effect. The one in each generation who places the highest value on philanthropy will dedicate their time, attention, and intention to the family's philanthropic cause.

The family member with the biggest drive to get an answer to the question of how the family can do good with its money is most likely the one who will give birth to a philanthropic cause or vision for the family. And, of course, every person will look at the world and perceive voids in humanity and society that resonate with their highest priorities and unique hierarchy of values. The vision for your family's philanthropic cause will be for the long haul. The vision is the starting point for the creation of the cause and is in essence the service offering to see people emerging from their past and living their potential.

Philanthropy is a nonprofit endeavor and needs leadership and people to execute tasks and functions. If you're the one who wants to get the family's philanthropy going, know that it will be your responsibility to drive and manage it. Here are some important points to consider:

- Surround yourself with the kind of people who will assist you in fulfilling your intention and vision.

- Do enough research and speak to other men and women who have experience inventing and bringing a philanthropic cause to life.
- Have certainty of your big *why*. The bigger your *why*, the more clearly your *how* will appear.
- Have realistic expectations and time lines. If you have unrealistic expectations and you expect support without challenge and pleasure without pain, you will create a nightmare instead of an inspiring vision and mission.
- Define a clear vision and mission for the philanthropic cause and legacy.
- Choose a cause that inspires you and ignites a fire in you. If you don't love what you're doing, you'll give up.
- Run it like a business with the right people in place, to whom you can delegate responsibility. Be an inspiring leader.
- Learn to say *no*. You will be bombarded with requests for financial support. Have clarity and certainty in your mind about the reason for your charitable aid or donations. Why do you wish to increase the well-being of humankind?
- Stick to your plan and direction and be authentic to your wish for making a difference to mankind.
- Be grateful that you have excess of financial means that give you the freedom and opportunity to be a blessing for other less-fortunate fellow beings.
- Be a wise custodian of the finances bestowed to your care.

If you're a family member of the second, third, or fourth generation or beyond and you have chosen to be the next person to take leadership and custody of the family's philanthropic cause, put the stamp of your vision and mission on it. For it to continue to grow like a snowball in terms of its influence and impact on mankind, you will be wise to consider the points listed below, but, most of all, make it the authentic expression of your vision and mission. If you merely take over the dreams, vision, and mission of your predecessors, you will lose momentum and focus. You are not called to take over. You are called to create more and bigger with what was passed to you.

- Learn from the successes and failures of your predecessors, but mostly learn from your own.
- Put your own thumbprint on the family's philanthropic cause. It is now your creation.
- Honor what was done before you and honor what you're adding and expanding.
- Surround yourself with like-minded people you can brainstorm with and to whom you can delegate responsibility.
- Remember the visionary—who is now *you*—needs people to help him or her execute and grow the philanthropic cause for altruistic and equally narcissistic reasons. The goal is as much to give you a meaning, purpose, fulfillment, and inspiration as it is to give meaning, purpose, fulfillment, and inspiration to the philanthropic accomplishments.
- Make it your act of love and an act of service—marked by your unique expression of transformative service and uplifting energy—that becomes a physical expression to benefit those less privileged than you.

Remember to own your social power and play as big as you wish to—for your own sake and the sake of others.

CHAPTER 8

The Wealth Creator Extraordinaire as a Health and Vitality Leader

An empowered person strives to be as empowered as possible in all areas of life. Empowerment is driven by your hierarchy of values and what you consider to be of high importance and priority. You'll be more inclined to focus on empowering yourself in the areas of life most valuable to you. If physical health and vitality is high on your hierarchy of values, it shows that you understand that your physical health and vitality are crucial to the execution of your dreams and vision for life.

If you do not currently place a high premium on your health and vitality, you'd be wise to ask yourself the following question: How would I benefit by placing a higher value on my health and vitality? You are born with one body, one pair of legs, one pair of arms, one pair of eyes and ears, one heart, liver, and spleen. Every one of your five senses and every one of your organs have to last a lifetime. Everything in your body has to last for your lifetime. The younger you are, the less likely you will be to place a high priority on physical empowerment (unless, for example, you play sports).

Your body is the vehicle that brings your service and vision to the world. The more you take care of your body and honor every part of it, the less your body will stand in your way, and the more your body will serve you instead of you having to serve it. Be an empowered member of the human race and follow common-sense physical guidelines for treating your body with the care it deserves.

Healthy Eating and Drinking Habits

There are almost as many different diets and eating styles as there are people. The secret is to listen carefully to your body and learn what works for you. What gives you optimal energy and focus to such a degree that food does not distract you and you're driven neither by hunger pangs nor the lethargy of a tummy that's too full? Regulated and rhythmic eating is the best. Discover what food and drinks ensure the optimal functioning of your body. Find the rhythm of your body's need for nurturance. Some people function optimally on regular, small meals. Others function better eating only when they feel hungry. Some need three meals a day, others six to eight smaller meals. The art is not to judge what your body needs for optimal functioning. It's rather the art of knowing your body, listening to the signals it's sending.

As an empowered person you'd be wise to abstain from harmful habits like the abuse of nicotine, alcohol, and drugs. Often, when you're young, you don't consider the impact of harmful habits on your body. But I can assure you that the impact will be felt as you move on in years.

Remember that a habit is formed through repetition and unlearned through repetition. Here is a proven and powerful process for you to follow in fighting and conquering bad and harmful habits:

1. If you feel a pull toward harmful habits, learn to understand the subconscious urge to submit your free will to substance abuse by

asking the following question: How is the substance serving me, and what are the benefits when I use it (cigarettes, alcohol, drugs)? List at least twenty gains you receive.

2. Determine which benefits of the habit stand out for you. For example, one benefit of smoking may be that it makes you feel connected to people; another may be that it helps you to make friends more easily. Now you have insight into your subconscious urge—the urge to feel connected, to have a sense of belonging.

3. The next step in empowering yourself and shaking bad habits is to find new conscious strategies in achieving the same benefits. Just be careful not to replace harmful strategies with other harmful strategies. Make as comprehensive as possible a list of new strategies.

4. List the benefits (at least twenty) of the new strategies and the drawbacks and negatives (at least twenty) of the old strategies.

5. Practice the new strategies until they become your new habit. Remember, even the expert was once a beginner.

You are your own biggest investment, and putting time, energy, intention, attention, effort, and perseverance in enhancing your health is a significant investment with long-term dividends and growth. Let's call it physical value investing with long-term results.

Do you know that your body weight is approximately 60 percent water? Your body uses water in all its cells, organs, and tissues to help regulate its temperature and maintain other bodily functions. Because your body loses water through breathing, sweating, and digestion, it's important to rehydrate by drinking fluids and eating foods that contain water.

Here are some important facts to know about water and why your body needs it:

1. Water protects your tissues, spinal cord, and joints. It keeps the tissues in your body moist and protects the spine and joints by acting as a lubricant and cushion.

2. Water helps your body to remove waste through perspiration, urination, and defecation.

3. Water aids in digestion, which relies on saliva, the basis of which is water, to help break down food and liquid and to dissolve minerals and other nutrients.
4. Water prevents you from becoming dehydrated.

The way to determine if you're drinking enough water is to look at the color of your urine. The clearer your urine is, the more hydrated you are. This is a good sign that you're drinking enough water. Remember, to the degree I look after my body, my body will look after me.

The Value of Exercise and Body Movement

Our bodies need to move, either as a part of an active lifestyle or as a structured exercise program. Movement is important for every aspect of our health. We are energy in motion. The benefits of physical exercise are numerous:

- It ensures ease of physical movement, because the movement of each specific aspect of the body is based on the philosophy of *use it or lose it*. You need to continually move so that you maintain the ability to move.
- It assists with internal movement. Movement directly impacts on cardiovascular function, muscle development, hormones, and pumping lymph throughout the body as well as aiding the return of blood from the extremities. The movement of blood, nutrients, oxygen, and cellular energy depends on our movement.
- It maintains strength in your body. Strength is developed and maintained by engaging muscles in activities that work the muscles and train them to hold, carry, and lift weight.
- It gives you more "get up and go" energy and increases your energy.
- It helps you to maintain your body weight.
- It's an excellent mood lifter and stress reducer. Endorphins, the body's feel-good neurotransmitters, are released during activity and creates a natural feeling of well-being and decreasing levels of stress.

Use the power of your mind to convince your body to move and do a form of exercise. Here is a mental exercise to do to help you to shift from inactivity to activity:

- List at least twenty benefits for you in doing physical movement and start to exercise your body in an active way.
- Think out of the box in terms of how you wish to exercise—dancing, walking, skipping, yoga, or whatever is of importance to you. It's important to move and get oxygen in your body and get the blood flowing.
- List at least twenty drawbacks for you if you choose to be inactive.

The Value of Breathing

Every moment of our lives we're breathing. It's a joy to feel alive and be filled with vitality. Breathing is our life source and is essential for our existence. We can survive for days without food and even water but only minutes without oxygen. Breathing happens mostly without our conscious awareness. Breathing properly is considered a vital part of our path to well-being. Although we seldom give our breathing a second thought, the way we breathe can have an impact on our physical and mental well-being. When we breathe properly, we reduce our stress levels and we boost our immune system.

In *The Breakthrough Experience,* Dr. John Demartini writes

> Physical life begins with your first breath and ends with your last breath. The quality and quantity of energy you receive, transform and generate is a reflection of the quality of your breath. When you have a balanced breath you generate great power and as your breath wanders so does your mind. As your mind wanders so does your breath. Balancing and centering your breathing will balance and center your mind. A balanced mind has access to enormous energy.

Your breathing adjusts according to your emotions. You stimulate yourself with inhalations and sedate yourself with exhalations. A good way to balance your mind in its fluctuating emotions is to use one-to-one breathing: inhale to the count of seven and then exhale to the count of seven. It is recommended that you breathe through your nose. You can also use one-to-one breathing to bring your body and mind into the present. Be aware of your breathing and use the art of quality breathing to enhance your life. Enhance the quality of your life by breathing rhythmically.

The Value of Rest and Restoration

Sleep is a wonderful and necessary break to take in your twenty-four-hour cycle. Sleep makes you feel better because you feel more alert, energetic, and better able to function after a good night's sleep. Investing in good sleep habits is an investment in your health, vitality, well-being, and performance. When you're young, you might consider sleep a waste of time. Although some people can function well on less than six to eight hours of sleep, most adults need between six to eight hours of uninterrupted sleep every night. Every person is unique, and you'll have your own unique requirement for the amount of sleep that rests and restores your mind and body. It's important to learn to listen to your body and become the best interpreter of the messages it's sending. If you're waking up feeling tired, feeling lethargic during the day, and falling asleep at night in front of the television, you're most likely not getting enough restful sleep at night. Know your body and learn to listen to its messages. That's what empowered people do.

A study from the Harvard Medical School showed the following important benefits that sleep gives:

- Sleep restores what's lost in the body while we're awake. Sleep provides an opportunity for the body to restore and rejuvenate itself.
- Many of the major restorative functions in the body like muscle growth, tissue repair, protein synthesis, and growth-hormone release occur mostly during sleep.
- While we're awake, neurons in the brain produce adenosine, a byproduct of the cells' activity. The buildup of adenosine is thought

to be responsible for the feeling of tiredness and as long as we're awake adenosine accumulates and remains high. During sleep, the body has the chance to clear adenosine and as a result we feel more alert when we wake.

- The quantity and quality of sleep have a profound impact on learning and memory. Sleep helps learning and memory in two distinct ways: A sleep-deprived person cannot focus attention optimally and therefore cannot learn efficiently. Second, sleep has a role in the consolidation of memory, which is essential for learning new information. When we're sleep deprived, our focus, attention, and vigilance drift, making it more difficult to receive information.
- Your body regulates sleep in much the same way it regulates eating, drinking, and breathing. This suggests that sleep plays a similarly critical role in your health and well-being.

More benefits of sleep include the following:

- It curbs inflammation in your body.
- It spurs creativity.
- It lowers your stress.
- It improves your general sense of well-being and fights depression.
- It helps you to win. A Stanford University study found that college football players who tried to sleep at least ten hours a night for seven to eight weeks improved their average sprint time and had less daytime fatigue and more stamina.
- Healthy sleep habits support longevity and quality of life.
- It helps with weight control. Researchers at the University of Chicago found that dieters who were well rested lost more fat—56 percent of their weight loss—than those who were sleep deprived, who lost more muscle mass.

The value of good sleep habits is part of investing in your health, vitality, quality of life, and well-being. Invest in developing your own healthy sleep habits.

The Body-Mind Connection

"Your physical body is one of the most amazing functioning structures ever to be discovered within the known universe," writes John Demartini. "It is the pinnacle of the expression of animation, or life. You could make a lifetime investigation of it and forever remain humbled by the mysteries it holds within its dynamic, intricate, syntropic, and homeostatic make-up."

You cannot separate your body from your mind. They're entangled in a beautiful dance, and whatever happens to the one has a direct impact on the other. The connection between your body and mind happens in synthesis and synchronicity. If you negate the one, you're responsible for negating the other equally in the same exact moment.

Take equal care of your body and your mind. You take responsible care of your body by the decisions you make daily about your eating and drinking habits, your decisions about your physical movements and activity, your breathing, and your sleep habits. You take care of your mind by equilibrating lopsided perception, applying life skills in shifting anger, bitterness, challenge, despair, and depression, and by choosing to take action to empower your mind.

I've taken care in explaining approaches and mindsets you can develop to enable you to empower yourself in all areas of life. Learn about and study the laws of the universe. These laws apply to every living and nonliving thing, to everything and everyone everywhere. Develop the habit of looking at life and every experience, every event, and every person with both eyes. Looking with both eyes means you apply the universal law of duality. I remind you of the wisdom of the Greek philosopher Aristotle: "A genius is a person who sees for every stressor there is an equal and opposite blessing."

Remember, maximum growth appears on the cusp of challenge and support, pain and pleasure, drawbacks and benefits, loss and gain. Nobody can escape the challenges and pain that being alive brings, but you can choose to develop the mindset and view of life that *you cannot choose what happens to you, but you can choose how you react and respond to what is happening to you.*

Invest in a healthy mindset and a healthy body with all you have and enjoy the richness and abundance of a healthy body and mind.

Is Gratitude the Key to Unlocking Happiness?

What do you wish for most in life? Most people will have a variation of the following answer: "I wish for happiness." Even Aristotle said every man and woman is in pursuit of happiness. But what if I tell you happiness is an illusion and pursuing happiness most often leads to perceptions of nightmares? What if the elusive *happiness* can be found in a simple act like thanksgiving and gratitude?

Gratitude is a celebration, affirmation, and recognition of the good in life. It doesn't mean ignoring the negative aspects of life; it's about acknowledging the blessings you're receiving. These blessings are to be found in both the positive and the negative experiences in life, since the positive experiences make us rest in our growth and the negative experiences make us grow out of our rest. Gratitude is available to everyone, everywhere, any time.

The benefits of an attitude of gratitude include:

- Gratefulness increases emotional well-being.
- Grateful people achieve more.
- Grateful people get along better with others.
- Grateful people pay it forward.
- Grateful people are less depressed.
- Grateful people are more resilient to trauma.

Gratitude is good medicine. For those who exhibited gratitude, the following have been observed:

- There is a reduction in perceived stress (28 percent) and depression (16 percent) in health care practitioners.
- Levels of stress hormones, namely cortisol, are 23 percent lower.
- Reduced feelings of hopelessness were noted in 88 percent of suicidal inpatients.
- Grateful people have 15 to 18 percent more efficient sleep.

- Improved inflammatory biomarkers were noted in heart failure patients.
- Risk of depression fell by 41 percent over a six-month period.
- Dietary fat intake reduced by 25 percent.
- Arthritis and irritable bowel syndrome patients demonstrated 15 percent lower depression.
- Physical exercise increased 25 to 33 percent.

Why does gratitude work? Gratitude amplifies, rescues, and connects, according to Robert A. Emmons, PhD, professor of psychology at the University of California (The Psychology of Gratitude, PPI conference in 2016). Gratitude amplifies and magnifies the perceived good in our lives. Please note that perceived negative experiences also deserve an attitude of gratitude because the negative experiences and the failures often bring out the best in people. Gratitude amplifies the value of future rewards (delayed gratification), and gratitude is considered to be the new willpower.

Gratitude rescues us from ingratitude, anxiety, depression, helplessness, and hopelessness. It takes the focus off ourselves. There are three ways of looking at life:

- Through the lens of abundance versus the lens of scarcity
- Considering what life is offering versus what life is denying
- Thinking of life as a gift rather than as a burden

Focus on what you've been given rather than what you're owed. Gratitude connects and is called the moral memory of mankind. It creates bonds between people and stitches things together. A little thank you goes a long way, but a little gratitude goes further. Consider the words of this forty-nine-year-old male with amyotrophic lateral sclerosis: "I believe that life is not always fair. It has certainly been true in my case. It's not fair that I should have wonderful, caring, supportive parents who raised me right, and brothers and sisters that are there when I need them. It's not fair that I should be blessed with a beautiful, talented wife and together we should have two equally beautiful talented daughters who make us proud daily. No, life is not fair. Why should I have had so many years of good health and energy and good friends to camp and backpack with through the years? ALS is a terrible disease, but it does not negate the rest of my life."

The Twenty-One-Day Gratitude-Habit-Forming Process

Follow the twenty-one-day gratitude-habit-forming process and invest in your body-mind connection:

1. Write down ten benefits and blessings of beginning the twenty-one-day gratitude-habit-forming process. How will developing the habit of gratitude enhance your life?
2. Decide on your *ritual* of practicing gratitude. Are you going to write it down in a book, blog, store it on your phone, or simply track your gratitude in your head? Choose how you're going to grow your gratitude habit.
3. Remember to be grateful for the challenges and support in your life. Gratitude is a celebration, affirmation, and recognition of the blessings you receive, found in both the positive and negative experiences in life. The positive experiences make us rest in our growth and the negative experiences make us grow out of our rest. Gratitude is available to everyone, everywhere, any time.
4. Plan a couple of minutes in the morning before you get out of bed and fill your mind with what you're grateful for about the day ahead. Test the saying, "What you're grateful for you will get more to be grateful for."
5. Set aside a couple of moments before you fall asleep and list what you're grateful for in the day that just passed. Fill your mind with thoughts of thanksgiving and see how it affects your night's rest.
6. Enlarge your thanksgiving circle of thoughts and ponder what you're grateful for about your spirituality—your vision, the meaning to your existence, and your life experiences. Whatever your form is of being spiritual, give thanks for it.

7. Focus today on what you're grateful for about your mind and the way you use your mental capacity. List the things you say thank you for, including mental experiences, opportunities, and what you've learned so far.

8. Count your blessings about the way you bring service to your fellow beings in your business, family, or community, and acknowledge your unique contribution to your world.

9. Everyone has a unique relationship with money. Practice gratitude for the lessons you've learned so far about money, how it gives you the opportunity to bless others, and provides opportunities for others.

10. No matter what form it takes, you're part of a family. Contemplate what you're grateful for about your family. Think of every member in your immediate and birth family and list what you appreciate in everyone, including yourself.

11. You're a social being, whether you have a big circle of friends or prefer a handful of close friends. Let your mind wander to your friendships and your social connections and think what you wish to say thank you for. Be the friend you wish to have.

12. You have one body, and your body works hard for you. Scan your health and your physical condition, and say thank you for what works and for what doesn't work. No one has perfect health; even if you have a chronic disease, be grateful for the blessings you receive from that disease. Fill your mind with gratitude for your physical body by listing what you're grateful for.

13. You live in a village you call your neighborhood and home. When you drive around, shop, or exercise in your village, what are you grateful for? Look for the specifics to say thank you for.

14. The more you moan and complain, the more you find to moan and complain about. The more you say thank you, the more you get to say thank you for. Contemplate the blessings of living in the country you're in now.

15. Warren Buffett says he has won the ovarian lottery, being born as a white American male at the time he was born. What ovarian lottery did you win?

16. Most people want to run away from challenges because they are, well—challenging. Yet challenges are beneficial *because* they're challenging, and when you change the way you look at them, your challenges start to look different. Choose a past or current challenge and write down at least twenty benefits of facing that challenge. Now list what you're grateful for about the perceived challenge and see how your outlook on life changes.

17. Loss and gain are two sides of the same coin. Looking at any loss in your life without equally looking for the gains keeps you a victim and disempowered. Your gratitude for any perceived loss will increase when you honestly look at what you've gained. For example, I've lost a substantial amount of money, but I gained a substantial amount of insight and knowledge about how to look after money wisely and focus on service and not on fantasies about money.

18. Gratitude amplifies and magnifies the perceived good in our lives. Please note that perceived negative experiences also deserve an attitude of gratitude, because the negative experiences and the perceived failures often bring out the best in us. Gratitude amplifies the value of future rewards (delayed gratification); it is the new willpower.

19. Gratitude rescues us from ingratitude, anxiety, depression, helplessness, and hopelessness. Gratitude takes our focus off ourselves. Decide today how you wish to look at your life from now on and be grateful for a choice.

20. Gratitude connects and is called the moral memory of mankind. It creates bonds between people and stitches connections together. List what you are grateful for about your relationships.

21. By now, you've followed the gratitude-habit-forming process for twenty days. What are you noticing about the impact of gratitude on your life? Where do you notice stronger connections because you've become more thankful for and toward people? Count your blessings for how the attitude of gratitude is connecting you more strongly to those you care about. Consider writing a letter of gratitude to a loved one.

Write a letter of gratitude to yourself. Write it in the first person and write it from you to you. Start it with "Dear XXXX, I am writing this letter today to express the deep gratitude I have for you. I am deeply grateful for—." I encourage you to include all seven areas of life and express your gratitude to yourself spiritually, mentally, vocationally, and financially and for family, social, and physical gifts. Gratitude makes you grateful for what you have. "Whatever you're grateful for, you get more to be grateful for," says Dr. John Demartini.

CHAPTER 9

A Conversation with Dr. John Demartini

Ilze Alberts: Welcome, Dr. John Demartini. I'm so grateful and privileged that you've made time available to have this conversation with me. We know your reputation as a human behavior specialist and polymath. For the last ten years, you've been one of the giants on whose shoulders I've been standing to learn more about human behavior. As a behavioral strategist for high-net-worth families, I want to talk about the from shirtsleeves-to-shirtsleeves in three generations proverb, or rags to riches to rags, as well as the challenges wealth can bring in families. I hope to inspire families and for families to tap into your wisdom to transform the proverb.

First if all, I want to make sure that everybody who's reading this understands what the proverb means, that the first generation has the big void and is driven to create wealth, put their energy, focus, time, and inspiration into growing wealth for the family, often creating a family business.

107

The second generation takes over the wealth, inherits the wealth, but doesn't really know anything about the wealth-creation process. It merely maintains the wealth. With the third generation, the wealth is all spent because the third generation is accustomed to an affluent lifestyle but not used to being productive to support an affluent lifestyle.

John Demartini: Definitely, I have worked with clients and some families that have had that challenge. In multigenerational wealth, this is often repeated. You see this over and over again, and it's a challenge because as you said, there is a void that drove the person to dedicate themselves to building wealth. They have a desire because they had poverty and challenge. They have the desire to give the best to their family, and sometimes they confuse giving them everything with helping them. They can actually enable them or disable them and make them dependent instead of productive and inspired. Then this just goes on and starts over in the next cycle, where the next generation is enabled, doesn't have a desire, and down goes the wealth. It's not uncommon and this is a very important thing because nature has a way of creating that cycle if a person doesn't understand the principles of wealth-building and how to sustain the meaning behind wealth-building and the purpose of it.

Alberts: John, I've spoken to many families all over the world, and it is true in the Western cultures and in the Eastern cultures that this proverb has been repeated for multiple generations. Why do you think it keeps on appearing in the same form? Why is this energy not being transformed? Some families so far have been very successful in transforming it. I think, for instance, of the Rockefeller family, but it's still an energy that keeps on repeating itself. Why do you think that happens?

Demartini: Well, as you said in the beginning, there are some individuals who have a challenging beginning. They may have come from poverty in some cases, and they swear they don't want to stay there. So they want to work very hard to do something that makes a difference and they want to earn as much as they can and they don't ever want to be in that poverty situation again. So they save and they have a very strong work and savings ethic. And then they learn gradually how to invest and start having money work for them, and as they do, they're inspired by the idea of building their wealth. It's meaningful to them, but there is that void that they had with the poverty that their children don't have, unless they're trained.

Many years ago, I had the option to watch a Forbes TV special. There was a very wealthy billionaire from England being interviewed, and he understood this principle and saw that he didn't want to repeat that history, so he made all of his children work and start at minimum wage in his own company. They were never allowed to go to another level of the company unless they had earned it and shown respect by all the other employees. So they had to work their way up and earn exactly what everybody else earned. They had to do every single job and they had to know the entire company or they would never be allowed to take over the company. So they had to learn every single job in the company. He believed that a billionaire was not a billionaire unless they were able to sustain it at least three generations. It had to be three because otherwise it's just rags to riches to rags again.

So he understood the principles and was making sure that the new generation had a work ethic and had a void and had to pay their own bills and take their own responsibilities and had need for wealth. So that's really caring for the next generation instead of supposedly caring for the next generation by taking away all challenges.

Now there's another wealthy individual who owned a hamburger company in America, a very famous one, and he made a statement when they interviewed him on that same show many years ago, saying he wanted to make sure that his kids never ever suffered a loss or lack again. His children did not have the same outcome as the other man's. His children ended up going into philanthropy because they had so much money, but they didn't go into working so they would end up spending their money, getting joy out of giving it all away. That's not a bad thing necessarily, as long as they're not giving it all away and starting all over. They're distributing the money, making a contribution to the world, but again they were giving it away and robbing somebody else of any accountability, the job of learning from trial and error. So what happened was they had so much money they didn't need it so they thought about philanthropy and then they were robbing dignity, responsibility, accountability, and productivity from people by just giving money to them. So though they weren't squandering money themselves, they were going into charity and then robbing other people of responsibility. So it was kind of "rags to riches to rags" in another way. It's so important to have an education around that because otherwise you automatically, as you say, dissipate it.

Now there is also a concern society has, which is the downside of multigenerational wealth, because if all of a sudden somebody grows wealth and the next generation grows wealth and the next generation grows wealth, you get monopolies in families. And so you can get vast fortunes and monopolies and then the money is not distributed through society. So somewhere between those two comes the mastery of making sure there is an accountability to grow wealth and wise management for the sake of society. There's got to be a balance between that narcissistic growth of wealth and altruistic service, with accountability back to the people.

Finding that balance is what I think many wealthy people are having difficulty with today. I know Bill Gates is facing that and Warren Buffett is facing that—learning how to find that balance and strike that balance, because without it, the situation just recycles itself.

Alberts: I've had the privilege of listening to Suzie Buffett, Warren Buffet's daughter, when we've gone to Omaha Week for the Berkshire Hathaway shareholders' meeting, and she has impressed me as responsible in her philanthropy. Since she is the second generation, I wonder if her father spent time on educating his three children on how to really create and maintain wealth, because that's what I find is the biggest challenge with the second generation. They grow up with the perception of wealth. They also know that they're going to inherit the wealth. What I've also found, which was a big surprise to me, is the wealth creator dies and there is the meeting where the will is being read and they for the first time find out that they're the beneficiaries of a big family trust and they never knew that they were going to inherit this kind of money.

So my first question is, why is the first generation often hesitant to even disclose to the children how much money there is, and secondly to empower them and educate them?

Demartini: Well, I just speak for myself, but I remember I was doing my estate planning a few years back and my kids happened to be in the office, so I yelled out loud enough so that everybody in the office could hear, "I want to make sure my kids know that they get nothing. It all goes to the Demartini Prize and Institute." Of course, I just wanted to make sure they understood they were not just going to inherit it. You can rob children of drive, so I made sure they knew that and I've made sure I've reinforced that. They're going to have to figure it out themselves. I will help them, but they're going to have to stand on their own two feet.

The next day, my daughter came in and said, "You know, Dad, I've been thinking about it, and I'd like to work in the family business." She made it really clear that she wanted to be part of it, to work for it in the business, and she is working for it. There is some hesitancy, I think, because I think some wealthy individuals sense and are concerned that if the kids know that there is unlimited wealth, they could rob them of that. So there is a concern about it, but if they educate them on how important it is to have meaning in life and to be productive in life and how that is an essential component of fulfilment in life, they can address that concern. Without this, money is without meaning. It's not the same as money worked for. Money that's from an investment does not have the same experience as money that is earned.

So educating them on that is the key, but if you're not educating them on that, you may be hesitant about letting them know you have a lot of wealth, because it may rob them of any drive and there maybe quarrels about it and maybe they'd even want their parents dead. Hurry up and die. I've seen that happen, so that is one of the reasons I think they hesitate—because they're not sure how to educate them. Multigenerational wealth training could be of great service to them because they may not know the ins and outs and what to do, how to structure that education, how to make sure there is accountability, how to manage it wisely.

I worked with a lady—her father built quite a large fortune, not into the billions but into the hundreds of millions—and he was an atheist. The irony of the whole thing is she ended up inheriting the money, giving it to religious organisations. If he had known that, he would probably have turned over in his grave. But she was giving it to religious organisations that were not really using it as the gift was intended. She finally woke up and realized she was giving money to organizations that were not doing what she thought, so she felt guilty that she had squandered the money. She didn't know enough about wealth building and she didn't know how to make it herself. She'd never worked in her life and she was just giving money away, thinking that was good. People who do not feel fulfilled and even have shame and guilt over not producing very commonly go in to altruistic contributions and form a charity to feel better about themselves. Yes, it's a good feeling to help people, but sometimes you rob people of accountability. In this case, she was actually robbing a lot of people of accountability in that spiritual pursuit, but she finally woke up and started managing money.

I actually had her make a list of what she'd done to earn all those millions, and when she actually looked at what she did, her decision about what she wanted to do with it changed. When I asked her to name the downsides of just rescuing religious groups, she started to see that she was basically robbing other people of accountability and forcing them to face a fantasy of what their life was. It was a great wake-up. She started managing her money wisely, and she started appreciating what that dollar was about and what she could do with it. She began to prioritize what she was going to do with the money, how to invest, where it would continue to grow, and how to use it, where she could continue to serve.

Alberts: That's a great example. So I'd like us to talk about our children. You have Alana, Breccia, and Daniel, all in their twenties. My children, Charne and Jacques, are in their twenties. How do you educate your second generation?

Demartini: My oldest daughter, Alana—she going on thirty-one—is working in the company, and I think she's taken on just about every role. That is, I think, to everybody's advantage. She really wants to take over. She wants to do some of the things I'm doing—teaching and coaching and counselling—and she's getting quite great at it, so I have a feeling that she's going to learn and master these things pretty well. She still has a long way to go, she's learning it, but she's definitely on her way to saving money. She's not only saving; she's learning how to invest. She has a drive for it. She's not trying to get something for nothing anymore. She tried that when she was a teen, but now she's realizing there's work involved and she understands what it takes to run a business—the challenges that come and how things are sometimes up and down because of economics and things.

So I think she's grounded now. It took her until her mid- to late twenties before she started grasping what it was about. So I've done some educating as I'm on the road with her, travelling with her, sometimes sitting down and having lunch with her. I do this a lot more because I intend to hand over some things to her, so I'm going to be doing more and more education as it goes along, but she is gradually doing it. If you give an education to them before they even need or have a reason for it they don't remember it, so now she is gradually taking on accountability. She's got a new apartment she's paying for, with more and more responsibilities, so she's understanding more and she's receptive to hearing things. You have to introduce accountabilities and responsibilities and productivities for them to feel the pressure of knowing what it's like to wisely manage money.

Now, Breccia is my middle child and she has her own company. She's in fashion and has a fashion company. I'm really inspired by what she's doing. She's very talented and driven, and she's starting to sell a lot of clothes, making some money. She has not learned everything about all the bills and its responsibilities and taxes, so there is a lot of complexity that she hasn't gotten to, but you can see every week and every month a vast difference in what she has mastered.

It used to be that I was part of the funding of the organization, but now she is self-sufficient and she's actually starting to make money. I don't hear from her that often so I'm seeing that she is now taking on more and I'm giving her feedback every time I see her. So I think she's a year away from being totally self-sufficient as an entrepreneur. And that's inspiring to me because that's what your dream is as a parent. You want to see that, you want to see them stand on their own two feet, and I believe that she's probably going to excel and make a lot of money. I think she is going to be very wealthy. She wants to take over Coco Chanel's position, and I really believe that she has what it takes to do that. So she is going to do well.

Daniel is younger, about twenty-five, and he just got clear about what he wants to do. He's been beating around the bush and I've always kept the door open in case he wanted to be involved in what I'm doing, but I didn't want to force it on him. But I wanted him to understand time is ticking, he needed to make a decision. So I told him, if you don't decide for yourself, you're going to have people pressuring you and pushing you because there is a basic law of Parkinson—that work expands to fill the time available for completion—and if you don't fill your day with things that inspire you, your day fills up with things that don't. If you don't learn to manage money wisely, you don't get the money to manage.

He's now on his mission and I've never seen him so inspired. I don't even recognize him because he was quiet and quite introverted and now he's really animated and talkative. He's really focused and he wants to contribute in the field of IT and technology with games. He's on a roll. So I have a feeling he's driven to make money. I told him last year, I just want to let you know my job is to get you completely independent by age twenty-five, and my expectation is that he starts taking command. It used to be at eighteen that was expected; now it's about twenty to twenty-five. I said my job is not to take care of you; you have to take care of yourself. I made it clear to him. All my children have clarity now that they have to be self-sufficient individuals. It's not my responsibility to take care of them; they can't rely on my money. I can't guarantee that I'm going to give them a penny; they have to earn it. If I saw that they didn't know how to manage money, I would leave them nothing. I want them to grow up.

Alberts: It must really be rewarding for you to see that they are starting to take accountability.

Demartini: It's more than rewarding, it's relieving.

Alberts: It's relieving, I agree.

Demartini: It's both. It brought tears to my eyes when I heard my son the other day, focusing on his mission. I just got tears of gratitude in my eyes. I think a parent has fulfilment watching their child find their inspiration, finding what they really want to dedicate their life to. So that was a very inspiring moment.

Alberts: I have the same experience with my daughter, who is twenty-eight. She bought 50 percent shares in a business and she came to us as parents and asked if we would loan her money. She has to pay it back with interest into the family bank, and it's really very inspiring to see how she's taking this very focused step to be an entrepreneur. But also the trend seems to be that your older children often are the ones to do this. Suzy Buffett said that to us. She said they didn't grow up with a billionaire father. "He was still just Warren Buffett," she said, "and we didn't know that there was money. We lived in the same house and we went to the same school and we drove the same car we had when we were little. We didn't have an awareness of wealth."

But the younger children often grow up in that more affluent lifestyle. I'm talking about the second generation. They seem to be the ones who often fall a little bit behind or take a bit longer. I'm thinking of a family I'm working with. He's now twenty-five years old and the young man said to me, "I know that my father is looking after me. I don't have to work and I know that when he dies, I'm going to take over the money, but I don't have a purpose." So his biggest struggle is how to find a purpose in life. How does he find meaning in life?

I also think of how my cousins came to talk to me. I have seven cousins. I'm the oldest of four children. They said, please teach us about empowerment. They'd hear me speak about this often at family gatherings and family dinners, about how important it is for the second generation to be empowered, so they said, please teach us. So I've arranged to run a retreat with them twice a year. The oldest one is twenty-eight and the youngest is thirteen, but it was a group decision to ask me to do that, so that was really inspiring for me.

Demartini: I think that it's essential to do that. I have a plan, when I get back to Houston, for a family pow-wow, because I have a situation where my first wife was not empowered financially. We divorced many years ago, twenty-some years ago, and she grew up in a family that was very socialistic, believing the government should take care of you and you should have people take care of you. I was more of a capitalist. I believed you work for your money and you earn it and you save it. So the family, the children, are now having to face this idea. Their mother expects her children to take care of her. She's perfectly capable of working, but she doesn't want to because she just assumes her kids should take care of her. This now puts another challenge on the kids, because what do they do if they take care of the mother? I have talked to the kids, and there is a part of them that doesn't want to have to do that.

Alberts: But they feel guilty?

Demartini: Yes, there is guilt if they don't do it, and there is frustration if they do—and resentment. That's one of the reasons we're having a meeting. I'm going to have to step in and state my view. I'm not married to her anymore and it's not my real responsibility, but I'm still part of the family.

Alberts: They're possibly still perceiving it as their responsibility, so what do you wish to say to them?

Demartini: My oldest daughter, Alana, has been taking on the majority of the crunch. She's been helping her mom, but now she's realising that she's enabling her. Her mom is not going to drive her independence. The woman took care of her parents, but her parents had some wealth, so taking care of your parents and living off their wealth is different from having no money and expecting your kids to take care of you. It's a different mindset, so there's going to have to be a reality check. All Alana's siblings are going to have to take part based on their own level of income. Potentially and gradually, maybe that will have to be remodeled according to the amount they're going to have to pay, say, if their mom is not able to work or choosing not to—because I believe she's capable of working. They must decide how they feel about that and share that with their mom and not hold back on what they're actually experiencing. They'll need to let her know what they feel, and if that's the case—that she's refusing to work—she needs to give a reason for that. And if they're okay with that, they're going to be accountable and responsibile for paying the bills, which could go up. I know the oldest daughter, Alana, is challenged by having to carry most of the load, because she's making most of the income. And she's resents it. She wants the other two siblings to participate, but they're hesitating. In fact, they don't want more income because they know they're going to have that responsibility. So it's an interesting dynamic.

I'm going to have to tell them that these are the responsibilities, so they have to speak up and negotiate with everybody and decide what they're going to do. The agreement may have to be renegotiated periodically, but they have to speak up and let everyone know what's going on because if they don't want to take care of her, then they may have to face the consequences of the mom not having an income. She has to understand that she has to either go to work or go on the street. So it's a challenging dynamic. But they have to be educated and it has to be rational, otherwise the resentment is just repressed.

Alberts: There are three young adults and it's wise that they make a team decision about it. Are you planning to sit with them and mediate a meeting?

Demartini: I see myself as directing the meeting so that it gets done. If I step in and rescue, that's not helping anybody. I'd just be put into a situation that's not even my responsibility ultimately. So I think the mother needs to hear what the children really feel, and I think the children need to know what the mother's reasons are. That way it's all on the table and wiser decisions result rather than assumptions. I think there has to be patience in some respects. Two of them are not earning much income yet and there's not much they can contribute, so the other one is overdoing it. So I think they need to know they're going to have to step up and play that role. I think it will be a great education for them and make them stand up and have accountability, which is great. Or it will make the mother have accountability, or perhaps a combination of the two. I'm hoping for a combination, where the mother earns some of her own money. Maybe she can't sustain all of her income, but the kids can take on some of it, so there's a nice blend, a family unit.

I don't mind participating in some respects, to assist them in the transition, but I don't want to be the rescuer. This is a factor that people have to understand, true value comes from truly serving a need. I'm in the family business and I do whatever is needed, but they have to produce. There has to be a fair exchange, and that's where the education comes in, having real equity and fair exchange in transactions. I try to educate people about maintaining equity and fair exchange. If there is no fair exchange, create change until there is fair exchange.

Alberts: John, one of my clients said to me, "The biggest curse of inter-generational wealth for me, and many other people, is the illusion that you don't have to do much with your life. You might want to and you might make the effort, but you don't have the same pressure to earn enough to live on, and that takes away a lot of the incentive to find meaningful work." Now you and I are both Baby Boomers, and they say we're the only generation that often has to take care of three generations: parents, themselves, and their children. The person who gave me this feedback was a member of the second generation, and as I was listening to her, what went through my mind is that she doesn't understand the key elements that give meaning to life. Let's talk about what gives meaning to life.

Demartini: I believe everybody has a set of priorities, a set of values in life. Those values are born out of the void they perceive. So if a person perceives that he doesn't have a relationship, he looks for a parent or a family member or a partner. If she feels like she doesn't have a service for the world, then she looks for a way to give service. If they feel they don't have money, they search for money. If they don't have health, they search for health. If somebody provides everything to them, it's all taken care of and they have no needs and no void that they're aware of. So they sometimes lose the drive to fulfill anything because it's all taken care of. They're enabled and this is why that void is missing, has no value.

The ancient Greeks used the word *telos*, meaning the highest value for an individual, the one that has the most meaning and purposefulness, the one that offers the most fulfillment. So everybody has a set of values, but if there is no big void in their life, there is probably no value in this life. If everything's been taken care of, they don't know what to do, so they look for something to have meaning, but they don't have any real need because everything is taken care of. That's the challenge. They don't have drive.

I consulted with a young man who was in his forties. His father was one of the wealthiest men in the UK, a multi-billionaire. The father enabled the son. The son didn't have any responsibilities whatsoever yet he had a fantasy that he was going to be like his father, this wealthy billionaire. But he didn't have any of the drive. He just wanted to party. He was a playboy teenager, when I met with him and consulted with him in London. He gave the impression of being sixteen years old, but he was in his mid-forties. All he wanted to do was party, play, and have a good time. And he was angry with his father because his father wouldn't give him the business. His father was getting close to seventy-five, and the son just assumed he should take over the business. I sat with him and he wanted to know what to do to get the business. I said, "I want to tell you something. You're not going to want to hear this." And he didn't. But I said, "If I were you, I'd give all my money back." His father had given him a large sum of money just to get rid of him, because he was annoying him.

And when he said just get out of here, he gave up on his son because the son was never going to be what he thought. So he had inherited this large sum of money. And I told him the wisest thing I could tell him to do, believe it or not, is to go and take all the money and give it back to his father or put it into an investment and leave it there and let it grow. "Then," I said, "go back and ask your father if you can work at the very bottom of the company, work your way up."

And he said, "I'm paying you money to tell me this kind of crap?"

I told him, "You can call it crap if you want, but I'm telling you what I advise you to do. The only way you will ever get your father's company is to earn it, and you have not done that. He's going to find somebody to earn the company, someone he believes will build the company and continue the company. You have no way of doing that right now. You spend your time as a playboy. So my advice is to take all your money and either put it an investment or give it back to your dad. Let him pay you with that according to what you produce and let him measure your productivity and you can find out what it is you actually like, what has meaning and productivity, because right now you have no dignity, no accountability, no responsibility, no productivity, nothing, and you're not going to do anything except blow money and he knows that. So he just gave you a sum and said get out of here. And you're angry at him because he's not giving you the company, but you don't know how to run a company." So I told him, "Do that. If you do, you'll have your company. If your father sees that you can run every aspect of the company, inside and out, and you've earned it, all the people from the company will respect you, and you'll have earned the right to the company. So you may have five years of work ahead of you to do all that—or longer—but you'll have a company in the end. If not, you're going to squander your money and you'll probably be poor some day, thinking you've been abused by your father. In some respects, your father didn't train you very well and that's the lesson, but right now you can't blame him. You have to look at yourself and ask what you want to do with your life. If you want the company, go and earn it."

Alberts: I hope he followed your advice.

Demartini: Well, he was angry when he left me, and I don't know what happened to him because I never got to see the guy again. He was insulted that I would say those things, because he was used to being looked up to and sucked up to by everybody. He was always the one with all the money and he bought friendship, but behind his back I think people had a completely different view of him.

Alberts: That's a complicated family dynamic that we often see—the father had the perception that he was right, the son had the perception that *he* was right. I'm thinking of a family that I'm working with now. The man is thirty years old, has been through many rehabs for alcohol and drug abuse. The father has been entitling him and paying for everything. So the father came to see me and said, "Change my son. I want him to work now." But the son said, "No, I don't want to work, not interested. My father pays for everything."

I look at these two and I think they have completely conflicting goals. If that were your son and you were the father, who had the wisdom to teach more empowering skills to your son, what would you say to him?

Demartini: The same thing I said to Daniel. I told him I lived on the streets when I was a teenager. My dad made me accountable at the age of nine, so I had my first little company at nine, and he made me pay for room, clothing, and rent.

Alberts: A wise father.

Demartini: I know what it's like to be on the streets so I have no fear about that. So I told my son I had no fear of putting him on the streets—to make him grow up and learn from hard knocks. I said, "If you expect me to take care of something for nothing, then just know that is not going to happen. If I see you're making progress toward your independence, I'll support and help you, but if I see you're just squandering things, I'm not going to pay for it. So you'll find out the hard way and if you want to be angry and blame me and act out, that's your choice. I'm not going to buy into it. You're not going to suck me into guilt trips, because they mean nothing to me. You're going to have to stand on your own two feet."

My son got that. He saw that, so he wants to earn money now. He wants to build his own life. I'm inspired by that because that means there's a drive there. I was curious about that, but I see I made it really clear that twenty-five was the turning point. He's twenty-five in December, so he's got three or four months to go, but he realizes he has to get his act together.

Alberts: We as parents, then, really need to have the skill of having a thick skin and not go into any guilt or altruism. We must know that what we're doing is really the best for them.

Demartini: Well, you're not here to be liked. You're here to be loved and you're being loved if you do that, because they will respect you when they stand on their own two feet. I guarantee if they get on their own two feet they're going to take you out to dinner and they're going to say, "It's on me. I want to pay for it." That is a very rewarding moment of their life when they can say *no, it's on me.*

Alberts: I had the first experience like that with my daughter when she took me out for dinner and said she'd pay for it. It really felt good.

Demartini: In the 1950s, I think that typically occurred between age sixteen to eighteen; by the 1980s, it was probably twenty to twenty-one, and now, by 2015, that probably happens in their mid-twenties.

Alberts: But research is actually showing it's more like age twenty-eight to thirty.

Demartini: Yes, it's in the mid-twenties to thirties. I see that. I think that's because we're living longer. So if we live to eighty-one, we will probably reproduce at twenty-seven; if we live to sixty, we'll probably reproduce at twenty; in the turn of the twentieth century, people were living to around sixty so people were reproducing at around twenty and they were getting married at sixteen to eighteen.

In the 1950s, there was a thing called an *old maid*. If a woman was twenty-one, she was called an old maid and nobody wanted her. She had to be married by sixteen or twenty, but today people are not getting married or having kids until almost thirty and even the late twenties or thirties. Everything is extended on because we are living longer, so I have to factor in that longevity factor, to put realistic expectations on it. I was already independent as a very young teenager, but because my kids have gotten some education, I extended that transition a little further, so I say twenty-five to thirty is the range. I expect them to be completely independent somewhere in that range.

Alberts: That is what the eagles do. They push their chicks out of the nest.

Demartini: Do they? Like I say, my father was a pretty wise man. I went to him when I was nine years old. It was summertime and I said I wanted to earn some money, so I asked him if there was anything I could do to earn some. He asked if I mowed the yard. Yes. Did I edge the sidewalk? Yes. Did I sweep the sidewalk? Yes. Did I sweep and clean out the garage? Yes. Did I get all the leaves out of the gutters? Yes. Did I clip the hedges? Yes. Did I pull the weeds all around flowerbeds? Yes. Did I shine my shoes? Yes. Did I clean my room? Yes. He said, "Son, I don't know anything else that needs to be done. Those are all the responsibilities for which you could potentially earn money and some of them I don't pay for anyway, so you're going to have to go to the neighbors."

So I said okay. I wasn't upset about it. So I started walking down the street and I found the Evans' house to be untidy. I could see there was work to be done in the yard and the garden, so I walked up to the door and said to Mrs. Evans, "Would you like your lawn mowed and edged and the hedges clipped and the weeds pulled?" She said yes and asked how much it would cost. "I didn't think in advance to figure that out, so I told her five dollars for the yard and this and that, and she said that sounded like a fair amount and asked when I could do it. I said I could do it that day. So I worked most of the day on the house and I made some money. I went out and bought a baseball and a glove and a bat. It really felt great to earn my own money and go out and buy stuff. A few days later, my dad said, "I see you got a new baseball and new glove. Where did you get that?" I told him I'd done what he suggested. I went to the neighbors and started earning money by mowing and edging. He wanted to know what equipment I used. And I told him I used the ones in the garage. "Son," he said, "there is a thing called depreciation and wear and tear on equipment, and since you used mine, you'll have to pay me for that wear and tear, because if it gets destroyed I have to buy another one and it's not fair for me to buy it when you're using it." I told him I understood, and he said I owed him seven dollars and fifty cents for the rental of equipment and gas cost. I told him I didn't have it, and he said, "Well, that'll teach you not to spend your money until all your bills are paid."

So I had to do two more yards just to pay him back with interest on the two new jobs as well. I was broke even after doing those two yards. I started doing new yards and making money, but I paid him and now I understood accountability. It was a little discouraging because I didn't make as much money and I had to work harder. But one day I was mowing and a boy on a bicycle stopped and he came up to me and we started talking. Finally, I asked him if he'd like to make some money. He did, and I said I'd pay him fifty cents to mow, fifty cents to edge, and twenty-five cents for raking and sweeping. He agreed, and I thought it was great. He liked the work, so he got two of his buddies to help and I had three buddies doing the yards with their own equipment.

Alberts: Three employees?

Demartini: Three employees. They were buddies, but they were employees. Then I got three more and then three more, and we used their families' equipment. The parents called my dad and found out how much he was charging me, so it was the same price. Anyway, I had this little business going, with three yard systems going on throughout the day. Sometimes I would get two or three groups, each with equipment, and I ended up paying everybody off for the gas and still made $45 for myself at the end of the day.

Now that was in 1963, and that would be worth about $700 today. So I was doing quite well. Many people don't even make that amount today. I bought myself a bicycle and a golf set. I started buying all kinds of stuff and my dad saw that every time I was making money I was just spending it, immediate gratification spending. And so he bought me a coin collection set and a little bank, the kind of bank you could put your coins in. I started filling it up with coins, because in those days people paid with coins.

So I filled up the coin collection set, and it became really inspiring to try to find those coins to fill up the whole set, because certain coins were worth more. I actually went to a coin collection meeting to see what the values were to incentivize myself, so I was no longer just spending the money. I was putting it into savings. My dad knew what he was doing; he was trying to get me to save, to think a little bit long range. He gave me the piggy bank, but he never did give me a way to open it, so in my office on the fifty-second second floor in Houston, Texas, in my credenza is the same piggy bank my dad gave me in 1963—filled with the same coins.

When I started doing that, I still made money on top of that. I still bought things, but I had the savings in place. One day my dad said he was proud of me for saving money, but he wanted to go to the next level of accountability. "I want you to know what it's like to buy your freedom," he said. And I thought, what's coming now, because every time he talked to me, I'd end up with less money to play with. He said, "I want you to know what it's like to have freedom, so from now on you're going to pay for your clothing, your rent, and your food in the house—$7.50 a week—that's going to be your responsibility."

I paused for a moment and took a deep breath. What was this going to keep me from doing? But I said okay. Then he said, "But you're going to have the freedom now to go anywhere you want on your new bike, anywhere, as long as you're home by nine o'clock."

So early in the morning, five or six in the morning, I would get on my bicycle and drive as far as I could—thirty-five miles in a new direction—to explore the city and then turn around and drive all the way back. I'd take a sandwich with me and just drive all over and get home by nine o'clock. That allowed me the adventure to expand my space and time horizon, to think a bigger game, and when my dad gave me freedom, he taught me that. That has been with me ever since.

I didn't do it the same way with my kids—I think I was probably too lenient in some ways—but that idea still stuck with me, how important it is. So I think that's a great gift. Of course, some people will consider that child abuse, child labor law defiance. In fact, one time I was telling this story in New York at a Learning NX meeting and a lady was offended. She said she wanted my father's contact details because she wanted to report him to child protective services. I looked at her and thought, what a strange thing to do, but I said I'd give her my dad's address. I gave her a cemetery plot, because he had passed away.

But she was irate because she thought his behavior was abusive. Yet I thought it was a gift. I look back now and wish I'd done more of that with my kids because I can see now that it would have sped up the process of their independence.

Alberts: That was truly a gift, John. You had a very wise father.

Demartini: Yes, but he also knew that I had learning disabilities and he wanted me to be street smart.

Alberts: That makes me think of the seven habits of highly effective families, or the seven habits of highly effective people. Let's talk about highly effective habits for a family to develop, to really grow a very powerful first generation, second generation, third generation, and into many multiple generations. As we consider the seven areas—spiritual, mental, vocational, financial, family, social, and physical—let's talk first about vision and purpose, because that is the starting point. That's what gives meaning to life.

Demartini: I wrote in my goal book—as you know, I have a goal book—many, many years ago, when I first started having children (this is a quarter of a century ago), there was one important thing I wanted for my kids. I wasn't always there because I traveled a lot, and I wasn't always able to be at the functions they might want me to attend, but the one thing that I found after reading Kahlil Gibran's *The Prophet* is that they come through you and not to you.

I thought, well that's true, because a lot of parents interfere with their kids and direct their lives so that the kids aren't even living their own lives. I wanted my kids to be free. My parents gave me a lot of freedom, so I told my kids if they needed my help I was there for them. If they didn't, I wasn't going to impose. But I believe they determined their own destiny. My one objective was to help them find what their mission was and then do what I could to get them moving toward it and achieve it. It was not to enable them, but to help them to achieve it, be a catalyst by giving them as much education as possible.

So that's why I'm inspired to see that all three of my children now have their mission. That, to me, is a very important thing for a parent. That was worth obtaining, finding out what that void was for each. Now all three are different. One had a void with clothes and fashion and it was evident at a very young age that she would go into that business. The other one was more intuitive and more education orientated, more philosophically rendered. She fit into my line of work. My son was the game player, wanted to make a living playing games, which is his business.

So I could see from young ages these tendencies emerging. I always kept the door open within my own company, because sometimes parents would love to see their children take over a company, but I didn't want to impose it. I wanted it to be natural, but now I don't care *what* it is they do, just *that* it is. Finding that is the crucial thing. I don't think that understanding is going to surface in somebody if they're enabled. It has to come from having frustrations and accountability, the void. If my dad is not going to take care of me, who is? I know my middle daughter started dating older guys for a while, whom she thought would take care of her. But she got burned by each one, and that was perfect, because she realized that they controlled her.

I'm very grateful that she went through those voids. Children have to be challenged. Our highest value, which is called the *telos,* is where our meaning and purpose is. If you're supported, you tend to acquire the values of others. If you're challenged, you tend to go back to your telos. It's the challenge in life that shows you your purpose in life, so you have to be willing to allow your kids to go through the challenges and learn through trial and error of their own. They have to go through it. We can guide them, but we've got to let them go and let them bang their heads against the wall a few times to get the voids they need to get going. There has to be a "dysfunctional family." In truth, it's functional, but it has to get them mad enough to go out and do something.

Alberts: You become the most innovative when there is a pain or a challenge or a frustration or a resentment that you want to transform.

Demartini: That's when you say I can't rely on somebody else for what I want to do. I saw that recently in a woman and her husband. The husband had a fling, and the wife saw that she had lived in sort of a pipe dream fantasy that he was going to take care of her. And as soon as he had a fling—and it was only a one-nighter, because he was not interested in a long-term relationship—she snapped and she realized that if he were gone she was stuck. So she immediately had a new void and determined she was going to build her own income source. The moment she did, instead of enabling the kids, she told them to stand on their own two feet. So the best thing that ever happened in that family dynamic was his little fling. It woke up the whole family, made the kids accountable, made the wife balance out the equation, not living in sort of la la land. Now they're closer than ever, but they've catalyzed the change. I've chatted with them and they tell me even though there was this illusion of betrayal for a time, they now realize that it was one of the best things that ever happened. It was a wake-up call. I believe things come into our lives to get us back to our highest values, our telos.

Alberts: So a good spiritual habit is to create voids.

Demartini: To create a void, to allow others to have a void. As I said, my parents dropped me off on the freeway when I was fourteen years old and I hitchhiked to California from Texas. I joke that I wanted to drop my kids off, but they kept coming home.

Alberts: John, let's talk about a good mental habit. I'm thinking of Charlie Munger, who has been Warren Buffett's best friend for many years. I listened to Charlie earlier this year, and he says the biggest investment you can make in yourself is to invest in your mind and to study human behavior. That's what you've dedicated your life to, so what would you say in that regard? What advice would you give to a high-net-worth family or to a family that's busy building wealth? What is a good mental habit to learn?

Demartini: I think that because a human value system underlies behavior, knowing the values and priorities of each member of the family is a smart move. That means knowing that the decisions they make are going to be based on what their values are, their highest values, because I believe every decision a person makes is based on what will give them the greatest advantages over disadvantage, greatest reward over risk. If you expect them to live according to your values, you're going to be aggressively betrayed. If you expect them to live in their own values, you'll be getting exactly what you expected and you won't be angry.

So I call anger and aggression, blame and betrayal, criticism and challenge, despair and depression, and the desire to exit and escape, the symptoms of a projection of unrealistic expectations on family members. You're going to want to change them, you're going to get angry and want to avoid them, and that can undermine relationships in families. So knowing the values of the family members and knowing how to communicate in terms of those values are very important. There is a great question that can help determine what someone's values. I have a value-determination process on my website. Ask specifically what their top three values are, what is most important to them. If you understand what their values are, it will serve yours because you'll respect them and communicate more effectively with their values in mind. If you think your values are right, like most of us do, and think other values are not, then you'll project onto them your values and expect them to do something and you will create conflict. Knowing what people's values are and knowing how to respect those values and communicate in terms of their values are essential—not only in a family but also in an extended family, in business, in society, among children, everything.

So that is a crucial habit to have, and I think learning and studying human behavior allows you to work in society more effectively, with realistic expectations. Parents expect their kids to be exactly like them, kids expect parents to be like storybook parents, everybody is projecting their values on somebody else and everybody is running into these snags. They're calling it a dysfunctional family, but it's not. It's just a lesson, and the symptoms are just feedback systems to teach them how to communicate. Charlie Munger is so well read and has studied human behavior and philosophy, and I think that helped him. I know it certainly helps me, because as I teach the Breakthrough Experience program, where I introduce some of these principles, I can see the impact it has on people's lives, when the doors open in their minds about what and how human behavior really works, not the fantasies. We fill our lives with a whole bunch of fantasies and delusions about how life is supposed to be instead of the way it is and the magnificence of the way it is far greater than any fantasy we will ever impose on it. So learning how human behavior works gives everybody an advantage.

Alberts: So a strong mental habit is to know value systems and study human behavior.

Demartini: Study human behavior and learn the art of communicating. When you're trying to sell to somebody in business and you don't know what their needs are and what their values are, you'll have a hard time selling anything. You won't be in business long. Well, we're all selling ideas to our family, and we're selling ideas about maintaining wealth. But if you don't know how to communicate in terms of their values, they're not going to buy it.

Alberts:　John, it comes to mind that a good vocational habit, which you so often say, is to love what you do and do what you love. Isn't that the best habit for your career or your vocation?

Demartini:　If you're not getting up in the morning and having a desire to go to work, then life is hell. And if you don't have a desire to make a difference in the world, then you're missing out on a life. I think it's innate inside us. It's part of the nature of human beings to want to make a contribution. So finding something that's inspiring and meaningful at work is crucial, and there are two ways of doing it. You either do what you really love to do and delegate lower priority things, or you link what you're doing to what is highest on your value system, so you can find meaning in it.

I try to teach both to people, because people are in different stages and sometimes they're in transition, between working for others and working for themselves, but if you don't find something that's meaningful, you'll have Monday morning Blues, Wednesday hump day, and thank God it's Friday every time. But if you do something that's meaningful, every day is Sunday. That means every day is a sacred day because you get inspired by what you love doing, and I think you don't age as much. You have more vitality in life. You have more meaning in life. I can't imagine going through life and not being of service to people. I think that is part of an essential component of fulfillment, so finding a career that's meaningful and not accepting anything less is essential.

Linking things temporarily as a transition is understandable, but stopping in mediocrity is unfulfilling. So find out what you love to do. I was having dinner at a Thai restaurant in Sydney, Australia, one time, and Tom Jones, the singer, was there. I was with my wife at the time, who passed away many years ago. We were having dinner and we joined him. And he told us that every day when he got up, he had a protein shake, worked out, got in shape, sang and practiced his voice. Then he did the next gig. He was doing 250 singing engagements a year, and he said he couldn't wait to get up in the morning and do another engagement. He said in the evenings he relaxed, had a glass of wine, and went to sleep. That was his routine, even if he was in a different country, he said that he loved to sing and he wanted to travel the world singing. He found what he loved to do and became a legend because of it.

Whenever you're doing something that's highest on your value list and you're sticking to the ABC's of priority instead of the lower priorities, you tend to expand your space and time horizons. You tend to have a bigger vision, you give yourself permission to go out and do something more extraordinary and make a greater contribution, and you're willing to tackle challenges and serve people more. You increase the probability of actually creating a legacy in life, leaving a mark in the world, which I think makes for lasting fulfillment. So I can't think of anything else more important in business than to make sure you're finding out what your highest values are and to make sure you're fulfilling your mission and sticking to your priorities. See if you can get to do the highest priority every day. Learn the art of delegating the lower priorities when you go to work every day.

Alberts: I just want to add, speaking to the mothers, that being a full-time mom at home is a vocation. It reminds me of Rose Kennedy. She said, "I'm raising world leaders." That job is a career, a vocation.

Demartini: I remember when I attempted to take on that role for just two days.

Alberts: I'm sure your children fired you.

Demartini: No, we had a pretty good time, but there were moments when I wanted to choke them. When their mother came back and took over, I was very grateful, because I realized I was not right for the role. My value system had trained me to do business not manage kids. Her value system was about kids. That *is* a business. The woman who has dedicated her life purely to the family, dedicated to the family, is in the business of producing a product—the children—that's going to be released long-term into the marketplace. She's also learning the art of making sure she does things that fulfill the husband's values, too, because he is probably paying for the activities she's doing if he's working and making money. She still has a responsibility to make sure she's meeting customers' needs—the husband is a customer, the kids are customers, and they are also products. So learning all that is still business, and it's still producing. It's just in a different for, but it's still production.

Sometimes women who don't understand that will devalue themselves relative to women who are out working outside the home. Now the downside of that, the vulnerable side, is that if she doesn't have an income source and something happens to the husband—say he dies and they don't have insurance—she's vulnerable if she doesn't have a skill. So it's a riskier arrangement, but it can be just as rewarding, as long as she is selling in his values and as long as he's taking care of his health, and as long as she's helping him get what he wants, then the whole system works.

That's how it was done up until the 1960s. The husband did this, and the wife did that. Today, we're more androgynous. The higher the social economics in a country, the more androgyny and the more male and female play both roles. But today women are giving themselves permission to do whatever they really want to do. If they want to be home and raise beautiful children, they have the right to do that. There is an art to it. If they want to work and have children, they have a right to that. If they want to do work and not have children, they have a right to do that. And I think it's great that they've given themselves that freedom now.

Alberts: So a good vocational habit is to love what you do and do what you love and, as Warren Buffett said, tap dance to work in the morning.

Demartini: Tap dance to work, yes. When people don't get that, I'm amazed. I've been in limousines and car services many times, and I ask the driver, so do you love what you're doing, and on occasion I'll find someone who says, "Yes, I love it." It's their family business and I get that. But lots of times they look in the mirror and they don't say anything. Then they finally look at me and say, "You gotta be kidding. It's a job, man. I have to pay the bills."

When I hear that, I say, "Do you mind having a conversation?" Usually, they agree and I say, "Is that how you want to live your life?" I start chatting with them, talking about what they really want. I actually had a guy start a company, doing what he wanted to do, as a result of chatting with him in the car. He was sitting there, unfulfilled, and I asked him what is his real love was and what was he doing about it. In that forty-five-minute drive, we worked to figure out a game plan and a business plan to help him get to the next level. And he did it; he started his own company.

Alberts: Let's look at good financial habits. We recently had a big family lunch, celebrating one of the cousins' eighteenth birthday, and as James Hughes writes in his book *Family Wealth*, the elders play a very important role in the teaching and educating of the next generation. I asked the men of the family, the first generation men, to give our cousin a word of advice, and Roelf, my husband, said, "Learn to pay yourself first and save, save, save." Isn't that possibly one of the top financial good habits to learn to have?

Demartini: In my particular situation, that was the turning point. I made a lot of money to buy things, but I didn't actually make the money work for me. I was its slave until I made a decision, around age twenty-eight, when

I realized I wanted to buy my freedom. I wanted to have money work for me, so I wanted to save it and invest it so I paid myself first. I did it electronically. I saved and kept increasing the savings. I did it methodically and lo and behold I was able to get to financial independence. It was not overnight; it took years. But it was very rewarding to know that I actually accomplished that.

Now you don't want to only save; you want to learn to invest, because otherwise the money will not keep up with inflation. But saving is a starting point because the second you have savings and you build it up, you'll want to learn about investing. As you learn, you become more sophisticated. As you accumulate wealth, you want to take care of it and see what you can do to make it grow. It's like a baby.

So that's probably the smartest thing to do make sure you find something you love to do, so you can't wait to do it. Make sure it truly meets people's needs. Don't project assumptions; make sure you earn an income. Make sure you save a portion of it, and pay yourself first. And learn to invest. You need to also learn how not to rob other people of accountability by rescuing them. It's a big challenge because a lot of people do that when they start to save money and invest it. People in their family or friends or whatever have emergencies and they bail them out and rob everybody of accountability. I've seen people save for four or five years and then a friend has an emergency or a family member has an emergency and they expect help. These people buy into the guilt trips and then they squander the money and never get paid back. Don't rescue desperation; invest in inspiration.

Alberts: So a good financial habit is to learn to pay yourself by saving, learn to invest, and to not rescue people.

Demartini: And then don't let your life go by, working your whole life for money. Have your money work for you; don't be slave, be a master.

Alberts: I can't think of a higher value in family relationships than to understand each other's values and to understand how your value is supporting and linking with my value. Do you agree that's a great habit to learn?

Demartini: Yes, it makes me think of a time many years ago when a man came to the Breakthrough Experience program in Columbus, Ohio, and said, "I wish my wife was here." I said, "Maybe next time she can come." But he told me he didn't want to wait a few weeks. He wanted to know now. So I flew back to New York, where I was living, and he flew his wife to New York to meet me two days later. And I spent the day in a hotel room with his wife, which sounds kind of interesting.

Alberts: And he paid you?

Demartini: He did. I was paid to stay with his wife in the hotel room. That's a misnomer, I know. But it's fun to joke about it. First, I found out what the problems were, because I was detecting challenges in the relationship, not major, but they were picking at each other. So I helped her identify what her values were, and I helped her identify what his values were and then I spent the morning linking those values. She couldn't see how he was dedicated to serving her or how what she was doing was helping him, so they were having problems communicating. We spent three or four hours doing nothing but that, and afterward, when we went to lunch, she said, "I'm actually looking forward to seeing my husband to try all this out. It's an interesting feeling."

"Before we go back," I said, "we're going to role play, and we're going to practice. It's like a sales training program. If you don't practice, you'll probably have to learn by trial and error." So we practiced, considering if she does this, how does it serve her, and if he does that, how does it serve her? And if she wanted something, how does she communicate that? Anyway, we spent the last four hours practicing how to communicate what she wanted in terms of what he wanted, and finding out what he wanted might serve her, so that she wouldn't be reactive. When you do that, you can love people for who they are.

So when it was all over, I got a letter—there were still letters written in those days—from the husband, saying he had no idea what I did with his wife in the hotel room, but wow, what a different wife he had. What I did was spend the entire day training her on how to get whatever she wanted from him in terms of his values.

Alberts: It's a great technique and a great skill.

Demartini: It changed their dynamic and I saw her at a few seminars for quite a few years after that, and it made a difference in the family. The knowledge spilled over to their children. They shared it with their friends and he used it in his work, and it helped.

Alberts: The important family habit is to know value systems and to do linking.

Demartini: Yes, because this thing is about a family, the summation of all the values in the family, counterbalancing each other. All the family values lead to androgyny, so if you have somebody that is very dedicated to saving money, you will probably also have someone who wants to spend money. If somebody is dedicated to a long-term vision, you'll probably want someone else who looks for immediate gratification. If you have somebody who's very intellectual, you'll probably have somebody else who tends to be intuitive. There are always these pairs of opposites in the family. If you can't master the skill of finding out how values that are the opposite of your own can serve you, you're going to want to project your values on others, and that is where all the tension comes from. Learning how to manage paradoxes is part of leadership, and learning how to manage paradoxes in families is part of partnership, and so mastering that is a really important skill.

Alberts: And what social habit are high-net-worth families wise to have?

Demartini: If there is a lot of wealth in the family, there are probably a lot of people looking at you. People find out about wealth and they want to know who you are. They're curious. It's like the way they react to celebrities. So you're going to be an exemplar of fine society.

I was in Hollywood a few days ago, and I got interviewed quite a bit about human behavior, about the celebrities, about their lives, and I was thinking, why can't they leave people alone? But people have this incredible curiosity about anyone who's either exceptionally wealthy, exceptionally successful in business, or exceptionally well known socially. It's like they live vicariously through other people. They're not building their own brands. They're living through other people's brands.

So with wealth come those accountabilities. And sometimes privacy issues arise so you have to deal with that as a leader; knowing how to manage all of that is essential. The wisest way to do it is to fill your day doing things that are the highest priorities. Decide what's the most meaningful, the highest priority, the most important thing, and stick to those every day, because if you have your day completely filled with most important things, you won't get distracted by the expectations of others. And your day won't get sidetracked by opportunists. You're busy, you're focused on getting things done, and you exemplify how to manage your life.

I think everybody knows that if you're not busy with something, strange stuff fills up your time. Never assume how much time you're going to have tomorrow. It's usually less than you think. Unless you set the agenda and turn away all else, unexpected things come in. You have to learn how to say no to outside influences and say yes to the things that are more important. Learn how to free yourself up. By doing that as a leader, you give other people permission to do the same, which makes for a more efficient society because they feel they have something extremely meaningful to do.

Let's say a young woman, who is twenty-seven, is about to get married. She has a wedding day two weeks away. Her discipline, her self-governance, her prioritization are extreme when she has a meaningful thing she's going to do. She won't overeat, she won't party too much, she wants to look her best because she's going to get into that dress. She's going to be focusing on that wedding and she's going to have self-governance because she has a purpose. But the same woman, if she doesn't have that wedding to focus on, if she has nothing going on and she's just existing, she will be more likely to overeat or maybe drink too much or do silly things. She won't be as productive.

So it's important to fill your days with meaningful things because when you do, your executive center in the brain comes online and you act with self-governance and mastery. If you don't, your amygdala comes online and you go toward immediate gratification, impulsive behavior, and addictive behaviors, and you end up not having governance. It's so important that our own physiology—our own life in general—gives us feedback to let us know how important it is to set priorities in life and have values.

Alberts: So a good social habit for high-net-worth families is to lead with inspiration.

Demartini: Lead with inspiration and prioritization and delegation and be authentic to yourself. That's called integrity.

Alberts: That is such an important one. The last one, John, is a good physical habit to have for long-term vitality and health. After all, this is my body, my vehicle by which I bring my service to the world. If I don't have good health and vitality, it's going to distract me. So what is a good physical habit for anyone with the intention to create wealth for multiple generations?

Demartini: Some of the same things we've been talking about also enhance well-being and health. If you're doing something you love every day, you're probably going to live longer. If you have a purpose in life, you're going to live longer. You'll have a will to live. If you do, you're also going to have more governance and you're probably going to eat to live and not live to eat. Gluttony is a foolish thing; overeating is a foolish thing. Irrational behavior costs you. Not having a routine, not having consistency, not having moderation cost you.

If it's not food, don't eat it. It's wise to eat quality food, something that has nutritional value that can fill your body with fuel and supplement your life. Most foods available don't have exactly what they used to have and it's wise to supplement. Drink a lot of water because it's better than stimulants, and breathe deeply. I call these the seven doctors have a great attitude; be inspired by reading inspiring things every day; get fifteen minutes of light a day (not much more because if you get too much you age and wrinkle quickly, but get a little bit of sun because you need some vitamin D); walk (I think people who walk live longer); have something to do every day that's totally meaningful, something that will last; set a goal for a hundred years at least (Paul Bragg, who lived to his nineties, told me to set goals to at least a 100 to 120 years. And I do. I have even longer ones). And make sure that you do a gratitude list every day. If you keep a document of what you're grateful for, your heart is more open, and you get even more to be grateful for. I think that that allows you to sleep better and have less noise in the brain and less distractions. So those are some things that I think help.

I also think that if you find yourself gaining weight, you're obviously eating more than you need, so use your physiology to guide you. I don't think I've fluctuated more than four pounds in the last forty years. I'm pretty much the same weight, yet I see some people whose weight fluctuates by twenty and forty pounds. If you're not doing what you really love and not having the executive center come online, you end up having these volatilities, so my advice is to stick to priorities and eat to live not live to eat. And make sure you drink a lot of water, breathe deeply, and get a little bit of light.

Alberts: So a good physical habit to adopt is to look after the health of your body and your mind.

Demartini: Exactly. Paul Bragg was the guy that changed my life big time when I was a teenager. He said there were seven doctors out there. One is the doctor of inspiration, and the other the doctor of perspiration. You have to work out a bit, eat quality food, and breathe deeply. All seven things I just mentioned are important. And also having work is important. You see people in their seventies and eighties who say they've retired, but if they don't have something meaningful to do, they go around asking, "Can I help you, can I help you?" They need something that gives meaning to their life, something that has purpose. If not, they decay. If you're not using your brain for high-priority things that are meaningful, your brain deteriorates.

Alberts: John, you've given us a wealth of information and I know it will serve many generations for hundreds and hundreds of years, and I know that the education you bring to us and to the world will continue to make a difference. I thank you for sharing the time with me.

Demartini: Thank you. I love doing what I do and I thank you for the opportunity for us to talk about it. I think the older we get, the more we think about the generations to come. I think that is the mission we both have now. Thank you for giving me the opportunity to talk with you and to help the next generation.

Alberts: Thank you, John.

CHAPTER 10

Principles of the Demartini Method: Based on Universal Laws and Truths

The following is a list of universal laws as compiled by Dr. John Demartini. He teaches these principles as part of the seminar he calls Breakthrough Experience. I wish to share his brilliant mind with you.

Principle 1

Your whole physical body and the universe are composed of vibrating, rotating, and translating units of energy-matter, which may be further broken down into subcomponents made of sinusoidal wave-particles condensed from frequency-specific quantum units of electromagnetic "light" and ultimately quantum fluctuating zero-point energy and Higgs's field. "It is the force we cannot see—the invisible

137

electromagnetic field—which is the fundamental force," said Richard Feynman. "It lies behind the solidity of everything we see."

Principle 2

Your mind, with its incoming ideas and outgoing thoughts, is also composed of or associated with vibrations electromagnetic "light" wave-particles. "Consciousness is an irreducible phenomenon, much like space, time, and gravity," according to *Scientific American— Penrose*.

Principle 3

Your ideas and thoughts are eternally conserved. "The master lives in a world of transformation," says Demartini. "The masses live in the illusion of gain and loss."

Principle 4

Your ideas or thoughts can be ordered (when balanced, grateful, and loving) or disordered (when imbalanced, ungrateful, and emotional). "Everywhere beneath the world's confusion there is an underlying order," said Murray Gell-Mann.

Principle 5

Your ideas or thoughts are either steadied (poised) by love or unsteadied (poisoned) by emotions. "Quantum information may exist only in the mind," said Christian von Baeyer, Chancellor Professor of Physics at the College of William and Mary.

Principle 6

Your ideas and thoughts, when unsteadied by emotions, will appear to oscillate or tic-tock. "Try to exclude the possibility of suffering, which the order of nature and the existence of free wills involve, and you will find you have excluded life itself," said C. S. Lewis, British novelist and theologian.

Principle 7

Your ideas and thoughts, when unsteadied by emotions, will undergo periodic emotional cycles—revolutions. Anything you don't love you will repeat until you love it. "Learning the game of power requires a certain way to look at the world, a shifting of perspective," said Robert Green, English professional footballer. "It takes effort and years of practice, for much of the game does not come naturally. Certain basic skills are required and once you master these skills, you will be able to apply the laws of power more easily. The most important of these skills—and power's crucial foundation—is the ability to master your emotions. An emotional response to a situation is the single greatest barrier to power. Emotions cloud reason, and if you cannot see the situation clearly, you cannot prepare for and respond to it with any degree of control."

Principle 8

Your ideas and thoughts can be focused wisely on balanced and loving actualities or unwisely on imbalanced and elating fantasies or delusions. "All things, including us, are made of fine-grained, strongly interactive positive and negative parts, all neatly balanced out," said Richard Feynman.

Principle 9

Your innermost ideas and thoughts maintain an overall balance of synchronous symmetry. "Complementarity is the most fundamental dynamic in our conscious constructions of reality," said Thomas M. Mandel, author of *The Operating Principle of the Universe*.

Principle 10

Your ideas and thoughts will synchronously spiral up and spiral down emotionally within a quantum, according to your hierarchy of values. Remember, there is nothing stable in human affairs; therefore, "avoid undue elation in prosperity, or undue depression in adversity," said Socrates.

Principle 11

Your ideas can rise and appear to come together (order) or fall and appear to go apart (disorder). "Some matter reveals itself by its luminosity, but all matter reveals itself by gravity," said John Barrow, English cosmologist.

Principle 12

Your ideas and thoughts, when emotionally imbalanced, initiate negative feedback loops from your four primary ecosystems to awaken your awareness to the ever-present synchronous balance of true love. "Nature never deceives us. It is always we who deceive ourselves," said Jean-Jacques Rousseau, the eighteenth century philosopher and composer.

Principle 13

Your ideas and thoughts can be *soul*fully alive in the present or appear to be *sense*fully living in the past and future. "We all start from naïve realism; the doctrine that things are what they seem," said Bertrand Russell, British philosopher and mathematician.

CHAPTER 11

A Conversation with James E. Hughes, Author of *Family Wealth*

Ilze Alberts: James, what a privilege to have this conversation with you during my visit to America, and I'm deeply grateful to you for taking the time. I want to first introduce you. I got to know about your work through your first book, *Family Wealth,* which you first self-published and then got published by Bloomberg Press in 2004. When I read the book, it opened up a window of new ways to look at families and how families generate and impact their wealth, how it moves from generation to generation.

I know that your book has been read by many people and you have written four more books. I know you're bringing out your fifth one soon. The second book published by Bloomberg was *Family: The Compact Among Generations*. What was the name of your third book?

James Hughes: The third one is *The Cycle of the Gift*. And the fourth is called *The Voice of the Rising Generation*.

Alberts: *The Voice of the Rising Generation* was written for the second generation, correct? For the generation taking over the wealth creation from the first generation? We'll be talking a lot about that in our conversation. And what's the name of the one you're writing now?

Hughes: It's called *Family Trust, Family Wealth and Wisdom: A Guide to Beneficiaries, Trustees Trust Protectors and Their Advisors*.

Alberts: I can't wait to read that, and you have one more book that's in the making, right?

Hughes: Yes, my co-authors, Keith Whitaker and Susan Lazansio, and I have committed either next year or the following year to writing a book called *The Wisdom Keepers: The Role of Elders in Families*.

Alberts: I'm convinced it's going to serve all of us who want to understand their role, so I thank you for your dedication and your willingness to share your wisdom with us. There are so many of us who are deeply grateful for what you've shared, and I would like for us to have a conversation about how we can help families to understand, first of all, the proverb, from shirtsleeves-to-shirtsleeves in three generations. I find it fascinating that many of the families I'm working with don't even know about the proverb, yet they're living the experience of it. When I had a conversation with you a couple of months ago, you told me the fascinating story of how in your early thirties you were called to go to Singapore. Please share that story, Jay. It's so inspiring.

Hughes: With pleasure. Imagine me sitting on the thirteenth floor of a skyscraper in New York City in an office of a law firm called Goodair Brothers and being one week away from a partnership election. I knew that my name had been put into nomination. Now, in the last few months of the year before you become part of a law firm, you tend to try and be as invisible as possible. So I was sitting there on a Tuesday and one of the partners came into my office and said, "Jay, we want you to go to Singapore on Saturday." I asked why. He said, "We have a client there who wants to talk to you." I asked if I knew him, and he said, "No, you don't. You've never met him."

"Charlie," I said, "you can't be serious."

"I am," he said. "On Saturday you need to be on an aeroplane."

"I don't have a passport."

"We'll get you one."

In those days, you could actually walk over to Fifth Avenue and in an afternoon get a passport. So I did, and I went home to my wife and three very small children and we got out an atlas to find out where Singapore was. Where was Daddy going? And on Saturday morning very early I went off to the airport and we flew and flew and flew and flew and flew and finally got to Singapore on Sunday afternoon. I was picked up by my resident partner, who asked me how the flight was, I said fine, and then asked, "By the way, George, why does this client want to see me? Do you know him?"

"No," George said. "We have no idea."

"Come on. You can't be serious."

"I'm serious. We don't know."

Well, I was beginning to get very agitated and anxious. So that evening I had dinner with two of his sons, whom I'd met in New York for maybe half an hour some months before, and I asked them the same question, "Do you know why your father has invited me to come?" They said no. "Does he do things like this very often?" I asked. They told me he didn't, that he was a very serious businessman and they didn't understand what was going on with him.

On Monday morning I got up and went down to Tanglin Road and went up to the seventeenth floor of the building. When I got off the elevator, there was nothing but a wall, and a secretary sitting there near a door. I said, "Hi, I'm Mr. Hughes."

"Oh, you are expected," she said. "Go through that door. So I went through the door and found myself in an enormous office, occupying the whole span of this large office building, and a Chinese gentleman was sitting at the end of the room in a chair raised up from the floor. In front of his desk was a tiny chair.

Alberts: Just one chair? Waiting for you?

Hughes: That was it, couches way off to the side and a big oil painting of a man I later discovered was his father. That was it. So I had to walk from where I was and sit in that chair and it felt like an eternity to get there. I did it. We shook hands and I sat down. He asked if I would like tea, and I thought, of course, in China I take tea, and he asked if I would like a cigar, so I said yes. I don't smoke cigars. And finally, he said, "Mr Hughes, you probably wonder why I have invited you to come." I said I did, and he said, "We Chinese have a proverb, shirtsleeves-to-shirtsleeves in three generations."

I couldn't help shouting back at him, "Yes, we have that proverb in my family, too!"

He looked at me and said, "Mr Hughes, I want you to tell me what the families in the West do to avoid this. I don't want my family to have this outcome."

"Well, I don't know," I said. "But if you would welcome me back in six months, I will give you the answer." He said that would be fine, and we shook hands. I felt much better. The walk between the chair and the door was now very short, because I was on my way.

Six months to the day, I went back and he asked if I had the answer. I said no, and he said he was very disappointed. "What I can tell you," I said, "is that in six months I've discovered that every culture on earth has this proverb, every single one. Rags to riches to rags, clogs to clogs, rice paddy to rice paddy, stable boy to horseman to stable boy. Every culture on earth has the proverb. I think what we must do is see—in the context of your family—how to avoid this outcome."

Then I said something that has continued to be in front of me now more than forty years: This fate cannot be overcome, but it's possible to avoid it. But every day of my life I'm still learning about this proverb.

Alberts: And you have dedicated fifty years of your life to seeking the answer to avoiding it. We had a conversation with a family earlier on, discussing the phenomenon for the second generation. The first generation creates wealth because there is something that has really driven them, a big void, but not so for the generation that follows. I'm thinking of a family I'm working with. The dad was fourteen years old when he left his country, Cyprus, to go to Africa, and he couldn't speak English. At the age of fourteen, without any family members, he arrived in South Africa and he had nothing and nobody, so his void, the emptiness in him to create something with his life, was massive. He is in his late seventies now and created family wealth because he had nothing and he wanted to build something for his life. That is typical the first generation.

The second generation becomes the custodian of the wealth and the third generation gets used to the lavish lifestyle. If there is no method or structure or foundation or a mindset or psychology being transferred to them, they make the proverb come true in their family. And that, of course, is happening in all cultures in the world. It's not only a Chinese problem.

Hughes: It's not just a Chinese proverb, Ilze. You've stated it beautifully. Many years ago I began a constant search for a way to provide a family with *intention*. That is a very important word in avoiding this outcome. It occurred to me that it is essentially no more and no less than one of the fundamental laws of physics. So if we think of that marvelous fourteen-year-old with all of his life ahead of him, with the courage to leave home forever, that is an enormously important existential act, a life act of existence. He not only had a dream, he also did something that was godlike with small *g*—that is, he made energy into matter.

The reality of our universe, though, is that the universe is all energy. There is a small amount of matter, smaller every time we measure it, and what we know is that families and the universe work the same way. Anything that becomes material must eventually go back to energy. Such are the laws of our universe. The great question of avoidance is the question of excretion of energy, because the proverb does not say when. It just says will. Now this is not subtle. This is very, very important, so I want to say it again: The proverb does not tell you when it will happen, because you do not know when the third generation will be in the proverb, it could be the tenth generation. All the proverb says—and mother nature is infinitely kind, she tells you it will happen—is that every family has free will as to when. And the question of when is constantly postponed. I have learned all over the world, from the families who don't have this outcome, that when they excrete energy, they make new matter. But the matter is not money; they make new, great human beings.

Alberts: Isn't that what true family wealth is? I know that when people talk about family wealth, they think of the financial wealth, but you and I both know that it is far beyond just the family's financial wealth. Wealth of family lies in the individuals, in the human capital.

I've incorporated the mindset and the teachings of Dr. John Demartini, the human behavior specialist and polymath, who has shared that there are seven key areas of life that generate family wealth. So true family wealth lies in spiritual wealth, in your mental wealth, vocational wealth, financial wealth, family relationship wealth, social relationship wealth, and physical health and vitality. You also—in your books and in our conversations—bring it back to the human being, the individuals of the family. The wealth lies in that. Please expand on that.

Hughes: First, I think Dr. Demartini's way of seeing and envisioning the multiple ways that we are and that our families are is to be celebrated. All too frequently, we fail to see that each of these aspects is a system. Each is an energy that becomes matter and each of them is in danger of the matter becoming energy. So a systems approach to each of them and the secretion of energy is the suspension of when.

Here's what I've seen, Ilze. Many years ago, I wanted to try to dispose of the word *wealth* because I believe that what it did in the brain was to immediately connect to financial capital money. Hundreds of times as I've spoken before audiences I've asked them to do a little exercise. I ask them to answer the question *What does the word wealth mean?* And, of course, people think I'm crazy. They always shout out *money* and *financial wealth.* I say, "Well, suppose for a moment you were sitting in the most beautiful place on earth, a beautiful, serene place. And suppose you have invited those you love the most to be there with you and they've come and experienced the place with you. Isn't that your wealth?" Now they see what happens in the brain and the heart as they connect two different brands. When you're in that serene place with those you love the most, you discover your wealth.

So even though I wanted to dispose of the word, I realized that it's the right word. To help all of us imagine what we're saying, I use a little hand signal. Suppose your thumb is financial capital, and suppose your first finger is human capital—all those human beings; and your second finger is intellectual—what you know, what you share; third is social—making good decisions together, growing, helping the world; and forth is spiritual, the spiritual capital.

This is what I've learned in fifty years. If the financial is the leading concern, the others disappear, just disappear. Now suppose you turn your hand upside down, and suppose now the financial capital is supporting the others. That is all it's doing, supporting the growth of our human selves, our intellectual selves, the social selves, and our spiritual selves. Now you're right orientated, now you're postponing *when*. So very often when I'm sitting with families or I'm with audiences and the question of wealth emerges, I just put my thumb up and not say a word and everyone goes silent and I watch the thumbs go down, quietly, peacefully, meditatively, reorientating.

Alberts: Going to the being of it and this is the doing of it.

Hughes: Absolutely. This doing is fine, but these beings are what change the *when* of avoiding the proverb.

Alberts: James, I've had many unusual encounters when I introduce myself and I tell people I'm a wealth psychologist. They immediately want to put me in a category, that I just work with finances. But I work with the wealth of the family, because I believe the ultimate purpose of a family is to encourage the fulfillment and prosperity of every family member. That has become such a nice analogy and a metaphor for me to use with them, so I thank you for introducing me to this. You also talk about the family balance sheet, and I've found that so useful in the work I do with families. We look at the assets and liabilities in the family, and I want to ask you to expand on that, because you've opened up a different way for families to look at their wealth.

Hughes: Thank you. When I was beginning to think about this and writing the first edition of *Family Wealth,* I appreciated that the generations would read the book differently. I was trying to find ways to illustrate to the different generations what I thought their tasks were. And I don't think I'm naive after this many years of being an outlier, because I realized that the first generation would be the most comfortable reading the book and the way we were discussing these matters. The dreamer would be most comfortable trying to use ideas in the form of accounting mechanisms.

So it occurred to me that there is no reason why one cannot manage and measure one's human capital. How do human beings thrive? Do they have dreams? Can they experience joy? Are they interested in a long journey? Can we establish our intellectual capital? Of course, we can. Every corporation on earth, including all these first generation men and women, are measuring their intellectual capital every day. In the world that we live in, can we measure social capital? Of course, we measure it by the quality, not the quantity, of the decisions we make. Are we making decisions together that are high quality, that are leading to higher ground? Or are we making decisions that are leading away from consensus? In our social capital, are we making gifts rather than transfers to the rest of the world? We can measure this.

Spiritual capital is also measurable, and we can do it without diminishing the extraordinary energy that lies in the spirit. What is the qualitative measurement of the spiritual capital? Do we have a common vision? Can we see our great-grandchildren flourishing? Can we understand harvesting the things that we've created in the natural way of life? We can understand and qualitatively understand our spiritual capital. So what I've realized, Ilze, is that it is quite easy to make a balance sheet of these five capitals and also express the liabilities.

Alberts: And what will be liabilities on a family balance sheet?

Hughes: Well, the first one is where we began our conversation, and that is that the shirtsleeves-to-shirtsleeves proverb will always be present. Mother Nature will always be standing there, and so the problem is us. That is a liability that never goes away, but then there are other things such as inadequate learning, inadequate interest in the dreams of the next generation, inadequate interest in the problems of the world, inadequate interest in making good decisions by consensus. There are all kinds of liabilities—poor health, the holocaust, external events—all of these I've seen great families manage. That doesn't mean they don't take losses in the fundamental sets of these capitals, but they are immensely resilient because they spend their time together on adaptation. They understand that any number of things can come from their own inadequacies. They're constantly asking themselves these questions: Are we adapting to our issues internal or external, and are we building resilience? Are we becoming our own best advocates because of the resilience of our system?

Alberts: It reminds me of the story of Max Planck. After he received the Nobel prize, he was traveling from university to university to speak, and his chauffeur would drive him around and would go into the venues and listen to his talk, and after he heard it about a hundred times, he said to Max Planck, "I've heard your speech more than a hundred times now and I can offer the speech myself." And Planck said to him "You're the speaker at the next event; I will sit in the audience as your chauffeur." And he gave the speech apparently brilliantly, and someone in the audience stood up and asked a question that the chauffeur, of course, could not answer. So he said it was such an elementary question that he wanted to ask his chauffeur to answer it.

Hughes: That is resilience and adaptability.

Alberts: The story makes me think that is, for me, the mindset of the second generation. They can so easily say they know it all, they can give the speech and they know how to take the family vision forward. But I've found in the families I work with that the second generation often builds up a resistance and even a resentment, perceiving that they're just the custodians of the wealth creator, the first generation's wealth creation dream and family vision and now they just look after that. Their vision, their own dreams for life have to take second place.

So Max Planck's story reminds me of that. I may think that I have the answers, but isn't it wise to keep going back and learning from the teacher who has learned in their own way how to create out of their own void. So is the first generation the teacher as well?

Hughes: Yes, in the sense of understanding the core human virtues of curiosity, creativity, willingness to suspend personal goals for a higher goal, the first generation represents a number of great virtues. Sadly, and we must honor what we've learned, the second generation comes to life in the face of those virtues, with a great deal of direction that they should practice these same virtues.

However, the shadow side of the first generation, and—as Freud and Jung and all the great teachers taught both of us, there is a shadow to the human side of everything—the problem with the first generation is that as it becomes convinced by its own success, forgetting those virtues, speaking them but forgetting them, it begins to believe that the only dream is its own, and that the task of those who come after is to store and conserve that dream. This is the shadow side of all of those virtues.

The second generation's great task is to evolve its own dreams with the help of its advisors, not at the expense of the first generation's dream but rather at the possibility of their own individuation and differentiation. Why? Because this is human, and this is what grows these capitals, rather than their disappearing in the face of this one. It is deeply humane, and yet, Ilze, this is the odd thing: By and large, no one cares about the second generation. The huge materiality of energy that has occurred in this creative, curious process becomes identified as that family, not they themselves. They become that, not this.

This is where the family energy begins to disappear, so it isn't that it's not important for the first generation's dream to be nurtured. What is important is that the people who are nurturing it are called to that work, rather than identified as children who must do that work. For advisors understanding this issue, the great balancing is standing apart from the first generation's dream and holding the second generation safely and asking what their dreams are.

Alberts: And give them the permission to live their dreams as well.

Hughes: Yes, and if we think about this in the most humane way and the evolving way of first individuation then differentiation, the gifts of the young, we come to the third stage of life, which is integration. Now, the second generation comes to that stage of his or her life, having brought a dream to life, been curious, been creative, done these things, he may be big enough now to deal with stewarding, but through the fusion in the high sense of his or her dream and the family dream, he can take a higher ground.

Alberts: It reminds me of the conversation we had with a couple earlier. He was sharing with us that he comes from a well to do family and he is third generation, and you asked, "Is your mother passing the dream or is she ruling?" And he said she was ruling. Now I know she's not intending any harm for her family. She is doing it out of goodness and because, in her perception, that is the best way. I believe every human being does what they believe is the best with what they have.

But the impact on the children is beyond what she is understanding, and I'm wondering, if we get the opportunity to work with a mother and father like that, what will we be able to help them with? That there is a transformation? You can't stop energy. You can't. It cannot be dissipated, but how do you help them to find a different way to do it? And how do you transform that energy when they say, "I'm buying into that because I can see the fulfillment and prosperity for me and for my children and beyond"?

Hughes: Ilze, this is one of the great unknowns remaining in my life, and what I think I can say at this point in my journey is that when family members, such as the mother of our friend, come to me in some grief, often sent by their children by the way, they do not come voluntarily. They ask me exactly your question, and the best answer I can give them is *What is your intention?* They usually give me what I would call a "nice" answer. Then I say, "I don't think so." And since I'm of a certain age and unlike almost anyone they've ever met, I don't care whether they need me or don't. I'm just there to be a voice. They realize that, and then they tell me the truth. And I say, "Well, that's good about your intention. You think you know better, you believe exactly in what you said—that if you pass this on, it's going to be very healthy."

I tell them, "The question, then, if that is your intention, is how are your children receiving it? After all, they came to see me and said I should talk to you. So how are they receiving it?" They respond, they're this and that, and I say, "No, no. Just for the moment, how are they receiving it?"

Well, that quiets things down. And then usually the person says, "What are you asking me?" Then I say, "What I'm asking you is how long have you been concerned that their dreams are inadequate? Or maybe you don't even know what their dreams are. Maybe you're closer to your grandchildren. As the Chinese proverb says, 'The grandparents and grandchildren are the natural enemies of the parents.' Maybe you know more about your grandchildren."

This begins a healthy, quiet, conversation. And what is the outcome? Well, this is all I can offer. The outcome, then, is this. I say to them, "If it really does matter to you, that the proverb is avoided, then you have to step out of this picture."

"What do you mean?" they'll say. I answer, "You have to become an elder. You will have to listen like crazy."

Alberts: And learn like crazy.

Hughes: I can't tell them that it will have a positive outcome, because I don't know how far the energy has already depleted, but I can be sure of one thing and that is that they will learn a great deal. I want to tell you that most people never come back, and that is fine.

Alberts: Because it's hard to hear the truth.

Hughes: It's almost unimaginable. It doesn't have a place in the brain, a connection to something, and that's fine. I never feel in the least that anyone is wrong. On the contrary, I believe in offering that kind of thinking and asking people then to consider it for themselves. I can do no better than that.

Alberts: That is a great question to ask. I don't always get the parents coming to me. I get the children, who come and sit with me and say they're angry, resentful, feel minimized. They feel all they are is the custodian of someone else's dream. So if we could invite metaphorically that gentleman in with us to sit down and have a conversation with him, I could help him in a certain way to change these perceptions and help him to see and own his own power and his own vision and his own dreams in conjunction with the first generation's.

How would you help the gentleman if he sat here with us and said my mother was ruling and had no intention of coming to see you because she believes that what she's doing is right?

Hughes: I believe in pictures. I think metaphor is how we learn, and I think narrative is how we express metaphor. In medicine, there is in America a very old idea that appears to be very new. The medical schools are teaching the new young doctors now that they must go beyond the first question, which is *What is your problem?* They must go to the second question, which is *What is your concern?*

If I ask a human being—and I have asked this all over the world many times—*what is your problem,* I will get a ten-minute response, and I could, in theory, fix it or not, depending on my capacity. But if I ask *what is your concern,* I know you will tell me your story. You will enter myth, not negative myth, white myth, living creative myths, and you will tell me your story. I begin to give you a way to understand your own problem as you express your concern, and almost always, in fact, at the end I can say—as we know from the great psychologists—is that in fact you already have the answer. They look at me and say, "How do you know that?"

I tell them I don't know that. They told me their answer. Underlying that, almost always, is that at no point in the life of the child—now fifty or sixty years old—did anyone ask this human being *What is your dream?* Ilze, one of the great tragedies of my life, one of the great, great sadnesses of my life, is that for so many second-generation people I've met, I am the first person in their life who ever asked them with an absolute open heart and open mind, *What is your dream?* In my family, I had an aunt who had no children—she was a gay—and she asked me and my brother and my sisters when we were fourteen or fifteen, *What is your dream?* She spent her life helping us bringing it to life.

Alberts: That is a gift that she gave you.

Hughes: An extraordinary gift. So it comes in odd ways, different ways in a family, but if someone doesn't care enough about you to ask you at that critical age, when you're individuating and learning about yourself, that critical question, *What is your dream? Who are you?* life will be hard. Without that love, life is very hard, particularly when you have money, because money is the most difficult thing to deal with. We know that from Freud, but if we don't learn to love, we can't learn to work.

Alberts: I want to add something to that—that we must also look into the mirror and love ourselves and ask ourselves, *What is my dream? What is the vision that I have for my life?* And how do I take my parents' dream and vision—whether I agree with it or not—and link it to my own? How do I take the snowball and grow the snowball?

Hughes: This is the essence of avoiding the proverb, because it is secreting energy. The energy of the new dream is not at the expense of another's. This, Ilze, is where, again, my conversations with a wealth creator often end, because the wealth creator's reaction is, "No, that would be at the expense of my dream."

Alberts: No, it is not.

Hughes: It is the absolute opposite.

Alberts: It's the expression, the continuation of it.

Hughes: In the Middle Ages in Europe, when a son was born to a king, the son would, after a short period of time, be taken away from his mother. She would see him occasionally, but he would have his own people from the beginning. When he got to be twelve, thirteen, or fourteen, the king would say, "Now you must have your own court, your own advisors. You must find your own friends now."

Clearly, the greatest threat to his throne was not the king in the next kingdom; it was his son making civil war on him if he stayed around too long. They were very smart kings, but they also understood that if the son did not individuate, did not discover in himself the courage, the various virtues necessary, he would be a terrible king. So these people understood human behavior remarkably well. They understood that if this person did not go on his journey—and by the way, the young women as well, but not quite—the next king was going to face different problems. There would be different internal issues, external issues. So this person had to go on his journey, and just as Joseph Campbell teaches us about the hero's journey. He would have to discover who he is and from there begin a real journey. Great kingdoms understood this, and when the king could not do that for his son or his daughter, often the kingdom collapsed. So we have marvelous historical pictures of how it works. We just don't pay any attention to them.

Alberts: But I just want to say again that genius lives in everyone, a dream lives in everyone, and everyone has the birthright to live that dream to the fullest.

Hughes: Ilze, it occurs to me in your beautiful statement that one of the things I've done in my life and I've made huge mistakes, huge mistakes. And I live with the consequences of them. But one of the things I did, after a very good mid-life crisis in a dark wood with nowhere to go, was ask myself, *Well if you believe in this question of dream, will you act it out?* I knew that first of all, I would be a fraud because I was not used to doing it. I wasn't sure I really meant it, so I began all over the world. To anyone I met, I said, "Do you have a dream? What is your dream?" And as I asked this question—*What is it to be human?*— I began to see that everywhere I went in the world, no matter the level of financial wealth or education, every human being has a dream. However, I also learned—and I believe this bears repeating—that the tragedy of my question was how often I was the first person who'd ever asked them. I was the stranger, the man of no country in a certain sense, simply wandering into the journey of my clients' lives.

Alberts: I must say that I find this session with a family member—whether it's the first, second, third, doesn't matter—when I sit and help them to connect with their dream, I find that to be one of the most inspiring sessions. I often find that I sit and cry with them, because it's so deeply touching to help a person to connect with the magic inside them.

Hughes: Yes, and I'm curious, so I'll make a statement and then ask you a question. After those remarkable sessions—usually the person has left and we have had an emotional goodbye—I sit quietly and I thank my spirit guides for putting me in that position, because I never know that I'm going to be in that position. Do you find that, too?

Alberts: I find that after a session like that, it's of utmost importance to me to go and sit quietly and go into that deep space in my heart, and express gratitude that I could witness another person's genius. That, to me, is such a gift and you never know that you're going to receive that gift. For that, I'm eternally grateful. That is why I can't stop doing what I'm doing, because of all the gifts I receive from my client and families I work with that one is the most rewarding.

Hughes: Thank you. Thank you.

Alberts: It reminds me of a seventy-year-old, also a first-generation gentleman, who came to me and said he made a huge mistake in his life. He spoiled his children, didn't teach them any financial skills, disempowered them. He said he had entitled them, but he knew they had a genetic predisposition, which was what he gave to them. "My legacy to them is my genes, and I think my genes are good genes," he said. I agree with him because he has shown them how to be a successful man. He has created a great empire for his family.

Yet, he asked me to please help him to change his approach to his children. And, of course, the resistance from the family members was strong. They said they didn't want things to change. I invited them in to a family meeting, and you know what happens when a family member isn't working from the bonds of affinity but from bonds of blood. There was resistance, there was anger. Around the table, I could feel the hackles were rising, but I'm so grateful for the questions I learned in your books *Family Wealth* and *The Compact Among Generations*.

So let's talk about that. How do you start a family conversation when there is safety? Please share your great way to have the family around the table. You know they do not want to be there and you bring in that reminder of bonds of affinity. Please explain what bonds of affinity are.

Hughes: *Affinity*, Ilze, is a remarkable word in English, and it's similar in all the romance languages. It's the word that describes positive connection—whether it's in chemistry, biology, psychology, in every academic subject—when you speak of affinity, you're speaking of some kind of positive connection.

Alberts: So it doesn't have to be blood relationships. It can be outside of that.

Hughes: Oh, yes. In fact, I'm going to say something that I think our audience is going to be a little surprised to hear: There has never been on the earth a family of blood, never. Every family begins with two names and two people who have nothing except their common humanity. There is no blood connection. As one of my teachers said, the only thing that's useful about blood is if you're in the emergency room and you need someone with your type. Otherwise, it's the worst place for your mind and heart to go because every family begins with a bond of affinity that two people have.

What is very interesting is that the first definition in Webster's of *affinity* is "relationships other than my blood." Affinity begins a family. We start from there. I will not help a family—I will not—if for whatever reason meetings don't begin with two names, if they cannot go back to how they started. As soon as a family puts two names on the top of the meeting, everything is already changed. For one thing, you've regained half your stories. You feel that now you have 100 percent of your narrative intact, and you have now intact 100 percent of all the ancestors from which the genetics come.

Second, I don't ask people to start with the most difficult problem. I try, purposefully, to start with something that's really mundane, to give people an opportunity to actually understand who they are again. So here are two ideas I use from time to time: The first is I tell them the first session is going to focus on the wealth creator and her husband or his wife, and the grandchildren and the middle generation are going to be quiet. They have no job here.

Alberts: They can be present but must be quiet.

Hughes: Oh, yes, but the only question is going to be from the eldest grandchild: "What was it like, Grandma and Grandpa, for you to be ten years old? Who are you?"

Alberts: Their job is to listen to the stories of the family.

Hughes: Everything changes, because no one remembers that they were once children. Isn't that fascinating? All I know is the head of the family is a colossus. They don't understand that these are human beings who had a childhood. What was it about? That is a great place to start.

Another wonderful place to start is to start differently. The way these meetings usually work, there is often a dinner the first night. Everybody sort of connects and then the agenda is for the next day. So everyone suspends their feelings for the next morning, so the dinner is simply contrived. I do something else. I say, "Okay, here is what we're going to do. Tonight is not just to say hello and get over your travel. We're going to find the biggest round table or create one ourselves, but we're organized in the dining room. The youngest grandchild, who is seven or eight years old, is going to go first, and here is the only question to be posed to that child: Who was the oldest person you knew in this family and what did they tell you about someone older?"

And now comes a story. You proceed around the table, with every family member speaking in order of age, and two remarkable things happen: First it gets very quiet and then laughter and then quiet and then laughter as the stories are told. Now one of the things that families forget is that the married ones are the only ones who chose to join the family. Yet no one knows his or her stories because there is only one dominant story.

Alberts: Because they are the outsiders.

Hughes: Yes, those are the only family members who chose voluntarily to join. As they tell their stories, they begin to weave a tapestry. What happens is the picture gets bigger. They now begin to actually understand what their system is. Also fascinating, by the time they get to the eldest, who today tends to be in their eighties, they begin to tell a story almost always of their grandparents and almost always something the grandparents told them about a great-grandparent. Now they're going back to a story about someone, often, who was born in the 1860s or 1870s, and all of a sudden they begin to create seventh generation thinking. They move everyone back in time, and realize this is their story, and no other story can be their story.

Now you can say to them, "Look what you've just done. You've woven your story now—120 to 130 years young—and these little ones are going to be a hundred some day. Look at your story. What do you want it to be?

Alberts: And when you listen to the stories of the previous generations, you know that you're a product of their stories. You're mindset, you're thinking, you're lifestyle are part of what someone else has decided in past generations. You see where you're coming from. That's why I love the word *bonds of affinity*, because that is a warm caring feeling. Blood bonds can feel threatening. I can help families by saying, "What is it that you wish for your family seven generations from now?" Now I've expanded a vision, whereas before they couldn't see it.

Hughes: And the people we would normally call the first generation, did you notice they disappear? They suddenly become the third generation of their own family or the fourth. The mystery of this, the mystery of narrative, is that there is a terrible triad in our field that says the stories of the family glue are trite. They're not wrong; they're just trite. What matters is that those stories are actually being told, so the narrative reality of how we learn to be human beings has to be taught. Stories are in our nature. They're what it means to be human.

So what happens in this very simple, gentle exercise is that people quiet down. They come with tremendous anxiety, and if the first meeting is about a big problem, everyone's anxiety will be high and everyone will have too large a chip in the game. They're playing for the final stakes instead of the way you play games. You start learning. You start with a little in the game, yes?

Alberts: And when you do that, there is a deep sense of belonging and anxiety calms down. So, James, I know that you have a wealth of wisdom, and I know that we can read more about that in your books and I'm looking forward to many more of these conversations with you. You've given us a wealth of information to go and work through, to think about, bring into our life. I hope other professionals reading this will be better equipped to help other families so that we can as a group of caring families, caring professionals, strive toward bringing out the best in every human being, helping every human being to live a truly fulfilled and prosperous life. Aristotle said we're all driven to pursue happiness, and is happiness not fulfillment and the ultimate prosperity in all seven areas of life?

Hughes: Namaste.

Alberts: Thank you for this conversation and for the heritage and legacy you're leaving for us.

CHAPTER 12

My Letter of Wishes for You

Dear reader,

This is my act of love to you. I've written and paved a way for you to build your generational family, with family members who are empowered in all areas of life. These areas of life include: spiritual vision and mission, mental genius and wisdom, vocational fulfillment, financial freedom, family connections, social empowerment, and physical health and vitality. I sincerely hope that you and your family will put the action steps in place to build your individual powerful lives and powerful families for generational impact.

The biggest investment you can make is not only in the smartest financial assets but also in the human capital of your family. I wish for you to hold the vision for your family and for you to live lives that are prosperous, meaningful, purposeful, inspiring, and powerful. The more you invest in yourself and in every individual member of your family to be empowered individuals in all areas of life, the more your family stands the chance to transform the shirtsleeves-to-shirtsleeves in three generations proverb so that it does not tell your family's story.

I believe it can't be the responsibility of a single person to defy the proverb. It's the collective responsibility of every family member, through blood bonds and bonds of affinity that move from generation to generation. Can you imagine the meaning and purpose you will experience if you live your life with a purpose bigger than yourself? Imagine looking back at the end of your life and witnessing a trail of loving and caring relationships, impactful businesses providing employment to many, mentally empowered decisions and actions, a body and mind that served you richly, a life purpose and vision that unfolded step by step, and financial wealth that enhanced the life of your family, your community, your society, the world, and the life you invested in for yourself. Imagine looking back with eyes filled with love and gratitude for every opportunity and every action step you took toward the fulfillment of your purpose and vision.

The most impactful action step a collection of family members can take to transform the energy of the proverb that tends to spells destruction and ending is to pour that energy into living with authenticity and truth to the purpose and vision of each individual family member of each generation, continuing from generation to generation. Be 100 percent true to your vision. Take action steps authentic to the expression and fulfillment of your vision for your life, and see how your vision and life purpose serve your family as a whole. Look far into the future how your decisions and your actions impact and influence generations to come, and know that you're essential and important in the big picture.

Be grateful for the part you play as an important member of your family. Be deeply grateful for your existence and for your family, and play your part with dignity, responsibility, and authenticity. Play big and make the best of what you have been given.

Follow the wisdom of wealth model I've put together for you all as your roadmap.

The Wealth Model

1. Unlock your wealth in all areas of your life—spiritual vision and mission, mental genius and wisdom, vocational fulfillment, financial freedom, family connections, social empowerment, and physical health and vitality.
2. Live your inspired life and have clarity of your vision, mission, and purpose.
3. Deliver the service you love to offer. Do what you love and love what you do.
4. Know your burning desires and have certainty about your dreams and goals.
5. Outline your action steps. The physical universe applauds action, not thought.
6. Focus on mastery. Focus on lifelong learning toward your own empowerment and self-mastery.
7. Have a grateful heart.

I know you have it in you to be the best you can be. I look forward to hearing from you as you journey through your life.

With love and gratitude,

Ilze Alberts

Afterword

by Dr. John Demartini

This book comes at an opportune time for many families who seek the answers to wealth preservation and transforming the from shirtsleeves-to-shirtsleeves in three generations proverb. I have been sharing information and research with my students for more than 30 years in understanding the laws of the universe and how to develop self-governance by using a method I have developed, namely, the Demartini Method. Ilze has been one of my earlier students in my South African seminars, and I watched her grow in her self-leadership in all areas of her life. She became one of a handful of Master Demartini Method Facilitators and through this book, my legacy is brought forward by one of my students.

Passing the Torch: Preserving Family Wealth Beyond the Third Generation is a book filled with practical applications and guidelines for every family member of every generation. Ilze mentioned to me a couple of years ago, when she started to focus on the niche market of family wealth, that I had introduced her to the book written by James Hughes *Family Wealth*. I mention this book to my students in my seminars as a great book on the topic of family wealth and the preservation thereof.

It came as no surprise to me when Ilze shared with me her intention to write this book. Her life, in conjunction with her husband,

Roelf, showed how they as a couple were showing up as the typical first generation wealth creators. In many of our conversations we discussed how to pass the torch to our next generation. This book Ilze brought to life is a testimonial of her dedication first to her own family and second to the clients she serves.

Money is a form of energy, and since energy cannot be dissipated, it can only be transformed. The proverb cannot be ended, but by developing the right mindset and human behavior, the energy of generational money can be transformed and preserved. In this book, Ilze gives guidelines on personal leadership and taking leadership of your families. She describes the essence of having clarity of your vision, mission, and purpose. She shares wisdom on mental and mind empowerment and understanding how to deal with the challenges and obstacles of life. She explains the importance of loving what you do and doing what you love and of offering your service to the world in your own authentic way. She gives guidance on how to manage money wisely. I have been privileged to buy a classic collection called *Book of Wealth* by Hubert H. Bancroft[1] and I have been sharing many of the insights with my students. I am grateful to see how my teachings have impacted Ilze and how she has made it her own in this book. Ilze has described a roadmap for families in building their strong relationships and connections as well as taking social leadership and building strong social networks and connections. She has included the value of taking care of your physical health and vitality, which makes this as comprehensive a book as possible on human behavior.

---

[1] Bancroft, H.H., 2012, *Book of Wealth – Book One: Popular Edition (Volume 1)*, Create-Space Independent Publishing Platform. The *Book of Wealth* was published in 1896. This rare 10 volume book was only printed 400 times. Bancroft distributed the book to the wealthiest people in the western world such as the Morgan's, the Rothschild's, the Rockefellers, the Vanderbilts, the Kennedy's, the Carnegies, the Fricks and the Fords.

Index